Longman School
Shakespeare

THE
HARRODIAN SCHOOL

Year book purchased:

YEAR	PUPIL	FORM	CONDITION

PEARSON
Longman

Pearson Education Limited
Edinburgh Gate
Harlow
Essex
CM20 2JE
England
and Associated Companies throughout the World

ISBN-10: 0-582-84871-7
ISBN-13: 978-0-582-84871-9

Printed in China
SWTC/05

First published 2004
Fifth impression 2006

The Publisher's Policy is to use paper manufactured from sustainable forests.

We are grateful to the following for permission to reproduce copyright photographs:

Donald Cooper/Photostage for pages 2, 3, 8, 9 (top), 10 (bottom), 11 (top), 13, 15 (top), 36, 37, 68, 69, 91, 100, 101 (bottom), 122 (bottom), 123, 157, 206 (top), 207 (bottom); Chris Davies for pages 15 (bottom), 122 (top), 156 (top); Ronald Grant Archive for pages 12 (top), 14 (bottom), 206 (bottom), 211; Michael Le Poer Trench for pages 11 (bottom), 207 (top); Photographer Jonathan Dockar-Drysdale © Royal Shakespeare Company for pages 4, 10 (top), 12 (bottom), 14 (top), 156 (bottom); Joe Cocks Studio Collection © Shakespeare Birthplace Trust for page 208; Photographer Malcolm Davies © Shakespeare Birthplace Trust for pages 9 (bottom), 90, 101 (top), 209.

Cover photograph: © Trinette Reed/Corbis

CONTENTS

ACT 1: SCENE BY SCENE

1 Don Pedro and his soldiers, who have just won a battle, arrive in Messina to stay with Leonato. As soon as they arrive, Benedick and Beatrice start quarrelling. Claudio tells Benedick that he is in love with Leonato's daughter, Hero. Don Pedro approves of this and offers to woo Hero for Claudio and to speak to Leonato on his behalf.

2 Antonio tells Leonato that he has heard that Don Pedro is in love with Hero and that he is going to propose to her that night. Leonato is amazed and delighted. He suggests that they should tell Hero and wait to see what happens.

3 After the battle, Don John has been forced to accept a reconciliation with his brother, Don Pedro, but he still wants to cause trouble. Conrade advises him to hide how he feels, but Don John says that he can't because being a villain is part of his nature. Borachio tells Don John that Claudio wants to marry Hero, and Don John immediately looks for a way that he can use this news to spoil Claudio's happiness.

ACT 2: SCENE BY SCENE

1 Leonato advises Hero to say yes if Don Pedro asks her to marry him. During the masked ball, Don Pedro talks to Hero. Don John maliciously tells Claudio that Don Pedro has won Hero for himself – Claudio is devastated. Benedick also thinks that he saw Don Pedro wooing Hero, but Don Pedro convinces them that he was trying to win her for Claudio, and the wedding is arranged. Beatrice has upset Benedick by teasing him while they danced together, but Don Pedro suggests that they would make a perfect couple. He asks the others to help him make them fall in love with one another.

2 Borachio suggests another plan to spoil Claudio's happiness and cause trouble: they could make Claudio believe that Hero has been unfaithful to him. Don John is pleased by this idea and promises to pay Borachio for helping him carry it out.

3 Benedick complains about how Claudio has changed since he fell in love. When he sees Don Pedro, Claudio and Leonato, Benedick hides and overhears them loudly discussing Beatrice's love for him which they have agreed to do in order to trick him. Benedick believes them and, when they have gone, he declares that he is in love with her too.

ACT 3: SCENE BY SCENE

1 To trick Beatrice, Hero and Ursula discuss Benedick's love for her, knowing that she is listening. She also hears them criticise her attitude towards men and marriage. Beatrice is upset that she seems so proud to others and decides to return Benedick's love.

2 Benedick is teased by Don Pedro, Claudio and Leonato about how his appearance and behaviour have changed. Don Pedro and Claudio are very happy that their plan to make him fall in love with Beatrice has been successful. Don John comes to tell them that Hero has been unfaithful to Claudio.

3 Dogberry and Verges give the watchmen their duties. The Watch overhear Borachio boast to Conrade that Don John has paid him well for his role in the plot to shame Hero. The watchmen leap from their hiding place and arrest Conrade and Borachio.

4 Margaret is helping Hero to prepare for her wedding when Beatrice arrives, claiming to have a head-cold. Margaret teases her for being love-sick over Benedick.

5 Dogberry and Verges tell Leonato that they have arrested Conrade and Borachio. However, their message is so garbled that when Leonato finally understands them, he does not have time to do anything himself. He is rushing to Hero's wedding, so tells them to question the prisoners themselves.

ACT 4: SCENE BY SCENE

1 At the wedding Claudio shames Hero by announcing that she is not a virgin. Don Pedro and Don John support this claim. Leonato believes them and is furious with Hero, who faints. Once the men have left, Friar Francis suggests that, to make Claudio feel regret, they pretend Hero has died. Beatrice and Benedick reveal their love for one another. Beatrice is furious with Claudio for shaming her cousin Hero, and persuades Benedick to challenge Claudio to a duel.

2 Conrade and Borachio are questioned by the Sexton and the watchmen reveal what they overheard about Don John's plot to shame Hero. The Sexton announces that Don John has run away and Hero has died.

ACT 5: SCENE BY SCENE

1 Antonio tries to comfort Leonato, who is devastated that Hero has been disgraced. They both challenge Claudio to a duel. Benedick enters and also challenges Claudio to a duel. Dogberry and Verges bring their prisoners, Conrade and Borachio, to Leonato. Borachio confesses his guilt. Claudio submits himself to Leonato, and Leonato commands him to marry Antonio's daughter.

2 Benedick tells Beatrice that he has challenged Claudio. They are then told by Ursula that Hero has been proved innocent and that Don John is the villain behind the plot.

3 Claudio mourns with Don Pedro at Hero's tomb. They leave to prepare for Claudio's wedding.

4 Before the second wedding, Benedick tells Leonato that he wants to marry Beatrice. Don Pedro and Claudio tease him. Hero, Beatrice, Margaret and Ursula enter, wearing masks. When Claudio says he will marry this 'new' wife, she takes off her mask, and is revealed to be Hero. Beatrice and Benedick publicly declare their love for each other. A messenger announces that Don John has been taken prisoner.

LEONATO'S HOUSEHOLD

LEONATO
Governor of Messina
He allows Hero to marry Claudio.
After her shaming, he oversees a
plan to ensure a happy ending.

ANTONIO
Leonato's older brother
He comforts Leonato after the
shaming of Hero.

HERO
Leonato's only child
She is publicly shamed when she is
falsely accused of being unfaithful to
her fiancé, Claudio.

BEATRICE
Leonato's niece, an orphan
She constantly quarrels with
Benedick, but later admits her
love for him.

MARGARET
Hero's gentlewoman
She is involved, without realizing it,
in the plot to shame Hero.

URSULA
Hero's gentlewoman
She gossips with Hero to trick
Beatrice into believing that
Benedick is in love with her.

THE WATCH

DOGBERRY
*Head Constable of
the Watch*
His mistakes and
misunderstandings stop
Don John's trick
coming to light
before the wedding.

VERGES
Dogberry's assistant
He tries to tell Leonato
about the arrest of
Conrade and Borachio.

MEN OF THE WATCH
Part-time police
They arrest Conrade
and Borachio for the
wrong offence, but
help to uncover the
plot to shame Hero.

OTHERS IN MESSINA

FRIAR FRANCIS
*The priest at Hero and
Claudio's wedding*
He believes Hero is innocent
and suggests they pretend
she has died.

SEXTON
*Church official who also takes
down statements from prisoners*
He sees the importance of
Borachio's evidence and
arranges to tell Leonato.

THE VISITING SOLDIERS

DON PEDRO
Prince of Aragon
He helps Claudio to win Hero
and he later supports Claudio
when he shames her.

CLAUDIO
Young officer under Don Pedro
He falls in love with Hero, but is
tricked into shaming her at their
wedding.

BENEDICK
Officer under Don Pedro
He claims he will never marry, but is
happy to discover that Beatrice loves
him.

BALTHASAR
Follower of Don Pedro
A singer

DON JOHN
Don Pedro's illegitimate brother
He remains angry with Don Pedro
and carries out the plot to trick
Claudio.

BORACHIO
Follower of Don John
He suggests to Don John the plot to
trick Claudio into shaming Hero.

CONRADE
Follower of Don John

Cheek by Jowl, 1998

Renaissance Theatre Company, 1988

RSC, 1990

RSC, 2002

RSC, 2002

RSC, 1990

Strand Theatre, 1989

RSC, 1986

Renaissance Films, 1993

RSC, 2002

Open Air Theatre, Regent's Park, 2000

RSC, 1990

RSC, 2002

Renaissance Films, 1993

RSC, 1996

RSC, 1982

LEONATO'S HOUSEHOLD

LEONATO *Governor of Messina*

ANTONIO *his brother, an old man*

HERO *Leonato's daughter*

MARGARET
URSULA } *Hero's attendants*

BEATRICE *Leonato's niece*

A BOY

ATTENDANTS

VISITORS

DON PEDRO *Prince of Aragon*

CLAUDIO *of Florence*
BENEDICK *of Padua* } *lords, Don Pedro's companions*

DON JOHN *Don Pedro's bastard half-brother*

BORACHIO
CONRADE } *Don John's followers*

BALTHASAR *a singer*

GENTLEMEN

OTHERS

FRIAR FRANCIS *a priest*

DOGBERRY *the Constable in charge of the Watch*

VERGES *Dogberry's partner*

A SEXTON

MEN OF THE WATCH *part-time police*

MUSICIANS

MESSENGERS

The play is set in Messina, Italy.

In this scene ...

- Don Pedro arrives at the house of Leonato with his soldiers and his bastard brother Don John. It is announced that Claudio has proved himself to be a good soldier in the recent battle.
- Beatrice and Benedick resume their habit of quarrelling with each other.
- Claudio tells Benedick that he has fallen in love with Hero, Leonato's daughter.
- Don Pedro offers to win Hero's love for Claudio.

A messenger tells Leonato, the Governor of Messina, that Don Pedro and his soldiers are approaching.

3 **three leagues**: about nine miles

5 **action**: battle

6 **sort**: kind / rank
    none of name: no-one of importance

10 **remembered**: rewarded
12 **in the figure of a lamb**: i.e. Claudio looks young
13 **bettered**: surpassed / exceeded

18–19 **joy ... bitterness**: he could not express his joy without weeping

---Think about ---

- What are your impressions of Leonato from these opening moments?

22 **kind**: natural

Outside Leonato's house.

Enter LEONATO *(Governor of Messina), his daughter* HERO, *his niece* BEATRICE, *and a* MESSENGER.

LEONATO	I learn in this letter that Don Pedro of Aragon comes this night to Messina.
MESSENGER	He is very near by this; he was not three leagues off when I left him.
LEONATO	How many gentlemen have you lost in this action? 5
MESSENGER	But few of any sort, and none of name.
LEONATO	A victory is twice itself when the achiever brings home full numbers. I find here that Don Pedro hath bestowed much honour on a young Florentine called Claudio.
MESSENGER	Much deserved on his part and equally remembered by 10 Don Pedro. He hath borne himself beyond the promise of his age, doing in the figure of a lamb the feats of a lion. He hath indeed better bettered expectation than you must expect of me to tell you how.
LEONATO	He hath an uncle here in Messina will be very much 15 glad of it.
MESSENGER	I have already delivered him letters, and there appears much joy in him; even so much that joy could not show itself modest enough without a badge of bitterness.
LEONATO	Did he break out into tears? 20
MESSENGER	In great measure.
LEONATO	A kind overflow of kindness. There are no faces truer than those that are so washed. How much better is it to weep at joy than to joy at weeping!
BEATRICE	I pray you, is Signior Mountanto returned from the wars, 25 or no?

Leonato's niece Beatrice asks mockingly about Benedick, one of Don Pedro's soldiers.

31 **pleasant**: entertaining

32–3 **He set up … flight**: He posted advertisements challenging the god of love to defeat him, i.e. Benedick used to boast that he would never fall in love.

34 **subscribed for**: accepted the challenge on behalf of

34–5 **at the bird-bolt**: to a contest with blunt arrows

38 **tax**: criticize

39 **be meet**: get even

41 **musty victual**: stale food
holp: helped

42 **valiant trencher-man**: hearty eater

43 **stomach**: appetite

45 **to**: in comparison with

48 **stuffed man**: i.e. a tailor's dummy, stuffed to look like a man

54 **five wits**: i.e. brain power
halting: limping

54–8 **and now … creature**: i.e. Beatrice got the better of Benedick's wit; she says that he is now barely more intelligent than his horse.

Think about

- How do you think Beatrice feels about Benedick?

- How far do you believe Beatrice's criticisms of Benedick?

MESSENGER	I know none of that name, lady; there was none such in the army of any sort.
LEONATO	What is he that you ask for, niece?
HERO	My cousin means Signior Benedick of Padua.
MESSENGER	O, he's returned, and as pleasant as ever he was.
BEATRICE	He set up his bills here in Messina, and challenged Cupid at the flight; and my uncle's fool, reading the challenge, subscribed for Cupid, and challenged him at the bird-bolt. I pray you, how many hath he killed and eaten in these wars? But how many hath he killed? For indeed I promised to eat all of his killing.
LEONATO	Faith, niece, you tax Signior Benedick too much; but he'll be meet with you, I doubt it not.
MESSENGER	He hath done good service, lady, in these wars.
BEATRICE	You had musty victual, and he hath holp to eat it. He is a very valiant trencher-man; he hath an excellent stomach.
MESSENGER	And a good soldier too, lady.
BEATRICE	And a good soldier to a lady. But what is he to a lord?
MESSENGER	A lord to a lord, a man to a man, stuffed with all honourable virtues.
BEATRICE	It is so, indeed; he is no less than a stuffed man. But for the stuffing – well, we are all mortal.
LEONATO	You must not, sir, mistake my niece. There is a kind of merry war betwixt Signior Benedick and her. They never meet but there's a skirmish of wit between them.
BEATRICE	Alas, he gets nothing by that. In our last conflict four of his five wits went halting off, and now is the whole man governed with one: so that if he have wit enough to keep himself warm, let him bear it for a difference between himself and his horse; for it is all the wealth that he hath left, to be known a reasonable creature. Who is his companion now? He hath every month a new sworn brother.

30

35

40

45

50

55

60

Don Pedro enters and is greeted warmly by Leonato.

62 **faith**: loyalty
63 **it ... block**: it changes with every new fashion
64 **books**: good books
65 **an**: if
66 **squarer**: brawler

70 **pestilence**: plague
71 **presently**: immediately

73 **ere 'a be**: before he is

81 **encounter it**: seek it out

---Think about ---

• What are your impressions of Beatrice so far? Think about the way she uses language and how she responds to the messenger.

86 **embrace your charge**: welcome your trouble / expense

MESSENGER	Is't possible?
BEATRICE	Very easily possible. He wears his faith but as the fashion of his hat: it ever changes with the next block.
MESSENGER	I see, lady, the gentleman is not in your books.
BEATRICE	No: an he were, I would burn my study. But, I pray you, **65** who is his companion? Is there no young squarer now that will make a voyage with him to the devil?
MESSENGER	He is most in the company of the right noble Claudio.
BEATRICE	O Lord, he will hang upon him like a disease. He is sooner caught than the pestilence, and the taker runs **70** presently mad. God help the noble Claudio! If he have caught the Benedick, it will cost him a thousand pound ere 'a be cured.
MESSENGER	I will hold friends with you, lady.
BEATRICE	Do, good friend. **75**
LEONATO	*You* will never run mad, niece.
BEATRICE	No, not till a hot January.
MESSENGER	Don Pedro is approached.

Enter DON PEDRO, CLAUDIO, BENEDICK, BALTHASAR, *and* DON JOHN *the bastard (Don Pedro's half-brother).*

DON PEDRO	Good Signior Leonato, are you come to meet your trouble? The fashion of the world is to avoid cost, and **80** you encounter it.
LEONATO	Never came trouble to my house in the likeness of your Grace. For trouble being gone, comfort should remain; but when you depart from me sorrow abides, and happiness takes his leave. **85**
DON PEDRO	You embrace your charge too willingly. (*Indicating* HERO) I think this is your daughter.
LEONATO	Her mother hath many times told me so.
BENEDICK	Were you in doubt, sir, that you asked her?
LEONATO	Signior Benedick, no; for then were you a child. **90**

When Don Pedro and Leonato move away, Beatrice and Benedick immediately begin quarrelling.

91 have it full: are well answered

92 fathers herself: looks like her father

95–7 If ... she is: i.e. Hero would not want Leonato's head on her shoulders as he is old and grey.

99 marks: listens to

102 meet: ideal

104 turncoat: i.e. something that changes sides

108 dear happiness: great stroke of luck

109 pernicious: extremely harmful

110 humour for that: frame of mind in that respect

114 predestinate: inevitable

---Think about ---

• Does Beatrice or Benedick come out better from their quarrel? How?

118 rare parrot-teacher: excellent repeater of empty words

120–1 so good a continuer: had such stamina

| DON PEDRO | You have it full, Benedick: we may guess by this what you are, being a man. Truly, the lady fathers herself. (*To* HERO) Be happy, lady; for you are like an honourable father. | |
| BENEDICK | If Signior Leonato be her father, she would not have his head on her shoulders for all Messina, as like him as she is. | 95 |

DON PEDRO and LEONATO move aside to talk.

BEATRICE	I wonder that you will still be talking, Signior Benedick. Nobody marks you.	
BENEDICK	What, my dear Lady Disdain! Are you yet living?	100
BEATRICE	Is it possible disdain should die while she hath such meet food to feed it as Signior Benedick? Courtesy itself must convert to disdain, if you come in her presence.	
BENEDICK	Then is courtesy a turncoat. But it is certain I am loved of all ladies, only you excepted; and I would I could find in my heart that I had not a hard heart, for, truly, I love none.	105
BEATRICE	A dear happiness to women: they would else have been troubled with a pernicious suitor! I thank God and my cold blood, I am of your humour for that. I had rather hear my dog bark at a crow than a man swear he loves me.	110
BENEDICK	God keep your ladyship still in that mind! So some gentleman or other shall 'scape a predestinate scratched face.	115
BEATRICE	Scratching could not make it worse, an 'twere such a face as yours were.	
BENEDICK	Well, you are a rare parrot-teacher.	
BEATRICE	A bird of my tongue is better than a beast of yours.	
BENEDICK	I would my horse had the speed of your tongue, and so good a continuer. But keep your way, a' God's name. I have done.	120

While the others go into Leonato's house, Claudio and Benedick remain behind. Claudio has fallen in love with Leonato's daughter Hero.

123 a jade's trick: a jade is a badly trained horse; the trick may be that the horse slips out of its harness.

130 be forsworn: have to break your word

139 noted her not: took no special notice of her
140 modest: sweet / shy

143 after my custom: in the way I usually do
professed: self-proclaimed
tyrant: i.e. critic

146 low: short
147 brown: dark-complexioned

Think about

• Beatrice says about Benedick, 'I know you of old' (line 123). What does this suggest about her previous relationship with him? What do we learn in this scene about his attitude towards women?

• What do we know about Don John so far?

BEATRICE	You always end with a jade's trick: I know you of old.
DON PEDRO	... That is the sum of all, Leonato. Signior Claudio and Signior Benedick, my dear friend Leonato hath invited 125 you all. I tell him we shall stay here at the least a month, and he heartily prays some occasion may detain us longer. I dare swear he is no hypocrite, but prays from his heart.
LEONATO	If you swear, my lord, you shall not be forsworn. 130 (*To* DON JOHN) Let me bid you welcome, my lord, being reconciled to the Prince your brother. I owe you all duty.
DON JOHN	I thank you. I am not of many words, but I thank you.
LEONATO	Please it your Grace lead on? 135
DON PEDRO	Your hand, Leonato: we will go together.

All exit except BENEDICK *and* CLAUDIO.

CLAUDIO	Benedick, didst thou note the daughter of Signior Leonato?
BENEDICK	I noted her not, but I looked on her.
CLAUDIO	Is she not a modest young lady? 140
BENEDICK	Do you question me as an honest man should do, for my simple true judgement? Or would you have me speak after my custom, as being a professed tyrant to their sex?
CLAUDIO	No, I pray thee speak in sober judgement. 145
BENEDICK	Why, i'faith, methinks she's too low for a high praise, too brown for a fair praise, and too little for a great praise. Only this commendation I can afford her, that were she other than she is, she were unhandsome; and being no other but as she is, I do not like her. 150
CLAUDIO	Thou thinkest I am in sport. I pray thee tell me truly how thou likest her.
BENEDICK	Would you buy her, that you inquire after her?
CLAUDIO	Can the world buy such a jewel?

Benedick laughs at Claudio for suddenly falling in love with Hero and tells Don Pedro all about it.

156 **sad**: serious
flouting Jack: mocking rascal
157–8 **Cupid ... carpenter**: i.e. tell outrageous lies (Proverb and legend said that Cupid was blind and Vulcan was a blacksmith.)
159 **go in the song**: fit in with your mood

169 **but ... suspicion**: who does not want to get married (Refers to the Elizabethan joke that the husband of an unfaithful wife grew horns.)
170 **Go to**: Come, come!
170–1 **An thou wilt needs**: if you must
172 **sigh away Sundays**: spend Sundays at home with your wife

176 **constrain**: compel

Think about

• What does Benedick reveal about himself in his responses to Claudio (from line 137 to 173)?

181 **your Grace's part**: the question you are supposed to ask

183 **If ... uttered**: i.e. If I had said this, that's how Benedick would have reported it.

BENEDICK	Yea, and a case to put it into. But speak you this with a 155 sad brow? Or do you play the flouting Jack, to tell us Cupid is a good hare-finder, and Vulcan a rare carpenter? Come, in what key shall a man take you to go in the song?
CLAUDIO	In mine eye she is the sweetest lady that ever I looked on. 160
BENEDICK	I can see yet without spectacles, and I see no such matter. There's her cousin, an she were not possessed with a fury, exceeds her as much in beauty as the first of May doth the last of December. But I hope you have no intent to turn husband, have you? 165
CLAUDIO	I would scarce trust myself, though I had sworn the contrary, if Hero would be my wife.
BENEDICK	Is't come to this? In faith, hath not the world one man but he will wear his cap with suspicion? Shall I never see a bachelor of threescore again? Go to, i'faith; an 170 thou wilt needs thrust thy neck into a yoke, wear the print of it, and sigh away Sundays. Look, Don Pedro is returned to seek you.

Enter DON PEDRO.

DON PEDRO	What secret hath held you here, that you followed not to Leonato's? 175
BENEDICK	I would your Grace would constrain me to tell.
DON PEDRO	I charge thee on thy allegiance.
BENEDICK	You hear, Count Claudio. I can be secret as a dumb man. I would have you think so; but, on my allegiance, mark you this, on my allegiance – he is in love. With 180 who? Now that is your Grace's part. Mark how short his answer is: with Hero, Leonato's short daughter.
CLAUDIO	If this were so, so were it uttered.
BENEDICK	Like the old tale, my lord: 'It is not so, nor 'twas not so; but indeed, God forbid it should be so!' 185
CLAUDIO	If my passion change not shortly, God forbid it should be otherwise!

Don Pedro and Claudio side with each other against Benedick's negative view of love and marriage.

189 **fetch me in**: trick me

190 **troth**: faith / truth

198 **heretic**: unbeliever
despite of: contempt for

200–1 **maintain … will**: keep up his pose of being a woman-hater except by sheer will-power

204 **recheat**: a call on a hunting horn

205 **baldrick**: a belt worn over the shoulder for holding a bugle

205–6 **shall pardon me**: must excuse me

208 **fine**: conclusion

212 **lose more blood**: Elizabethans believed that love-sick sighs drained blood from the heart but wine would restore it.

214 **ballad-maker**: one who writes love songs

215 **for … Cupid**: as a brothel sign

217 **notable argument**: outstanding subject for discussion

218 **bottle**: wicker basket, here, used for target practice

220 **Adam**: a famous archer

Think about

- Lines 204 to 205 refer to a popular Elizabethan joke based on the idea that a cuckold (the husband of an unfaithful wife) grew horns. As you read the play, be alert to the jokes about horns. Who seems most concerned here about becoming a cuckold?

DON PEDRO	Amen, if you love her; for the lady is very well worthy.
CLAUDIO	You speak this to fetch me in, my lord.
DON PEDRO	By my troth, I speak my thought. 190
CLAUDIO	And in faith, my lord, I spoke mine.
BENEDICK	And by my two faiths and troths, my lord, I spoke mine.
CLAUDIO	That I love her, I feel.
DON PEDRO	That she is worthy, I know.
BENEDICK	That I neither feel how she should be loved, nor know 195 how she should be worthy, is the opinion that fire cannot melt out of me. I will die in it at the stake.
DON PEDRO	Thou wast ever an obstinate heretic in the despite of beauty.
CLAUDIO	And never could maintain his part but in the force of his 200 will.
BENEDICK	That a woman conceived me, I thank her: that she brought me up, I likewise give her most humble thanks. But that I will have a recheat winded in my forehead, or hang my bugle in an invisible baldrick, all women shall 205 pardon me. Because I will not do them the wrong to mistrust any, I will do myself the right to trust none: and the fine is, for the which I may go the finer, I will live a bachelor.
DON PEDRO	I shall see thee, ere I die, look pale with love. 210
BENEDICK	With anger, with sickness, or with hunger, my lord, not with love. Prove that ever I lose more blood with love than I will get again with drinking, pick out mine eyes with a ballad-maker's pen, and hang me up at the door of a brothel-house for the sign of blind Cupid. 215
DON PEDRO	Well, if ever thou dost fall from this faith, thou wilt prove a notable argument.
BENEDICK	If I do, hang me in a bottle like a cat, and shoot at me; and he that hits me, let him be clapped on the shoulder, and called Adam. 220

31

Don Pedro asks Benedick to go and tell Leonato that he will return for dinner. Claudio asks Don Pedro for his support in winning Hero.

221 **as time shall try**: time will tell

221–2 **'In time ... yoke'**: i.e. even the wildest beast can be tamed

229 **horn-mad**: stark mad (with an obvious reference to the cuckold's horns)

230 **spent all his quiver**: used up all his arrows, i.e. done all his work
   Venice: a city noted for sexual immorality

233 **temporize with the hours**: change your ways over time

237 **matter**: substance

238 **embassage**: mission / task
   and so I commit you: a conventional form of closing letters

242 **guarded with fragments**: decorated with scraps

241–2 **the guards ... basted on**: i.e. the decorative words have little connection to the point

243 **flout old ends**: mock conventional phrases

247 **apt**: quick

251 **affect**: love

Think about

- At line 245 there is a change from prose to verse/poetry. What is the effect of this?

32

DON PEDRO	Well, as time shall try: 'In time the savage bull doth bear the yoke.'
BENEDICK	The savage bull may: but if ever the sensible Benedick bear it, pluck off the bull's horns and set them in my forehead, and let me be vilely painted – and, in such 225 great letters as they write 'Here is good horse to hire', let them signify under my sign 'Here you may see Benedick, the married man.'
CLAUDIO	If this should ever happen, thou wouldst be horn-mad.
DON PEDRO	Nay, if Cupid have not spent all his quiver in Venice, 230 thou wilt quake for this shortly.
BENEDICK	I look for an earthquake too, then.
DON PEDRO	Well, you will temporize with the hours. In the meantime, good Signior Benedick, repair to Leonato's, commend me to him, and tell him I will not fail him at 235 supper; for indeed he hath made great preparation.
BENEDICK	I have almost matter enough in me for such an embassage; and so I commit you –
CLAUDIO	To the tuition of God. From my house, if I had it –
DON PEDRO	The sixth of July. Your loving friend, Benedick. 240
BENEDICK	Nay, mock not, mock not. The body of your discourse is sometime guarded with fragments, and the guards are but slightly basted on neither. Ere you flout old ends any further, examine your conscience: and so I leave you.

Exit.

CLAUDIO	My liege, your Highness now may do me good. 245
DON PEDRO	My love is thine to teach. Teach it but how, And thou shalt see how apt it is to learn Any hard lesson that may do thee good.
CLAUDIO	Hath Leonato any son, my lord?
DON PEDRO	No child but Hero: she's his only heir. 250 Dost thou affect her, Claudio?

Don Pedro approves the match. He offers to win Hero for Claudio and to talk to Leonato about it.

252 **ended action**: recent battle

264 **break with**: broach the subject to

268 **complexion**: appearance
270 **salved**: softened
treatise: discussion

272 **The fairest ... necessity**: The best gift is the one that fulfils the need.
273 **Look what**: Whatever
'Tis ... lovest: 1 in short you're in love; 2 you fall in love only once
274 **fit thee**: provide you

Think about

- Why do you think Don Pedro might have offered to win Hero for Claudio?

- What are your impressions of Claudio and Don Pedro at the end of this scene?

CLAUDIO	O my lord,
	When you went onward on this ended action,
	I looked upon her with a soldier's eye,
	That liked, but had a rougher task in hand
	Than to drive liking to the name of love.	255
	But now I am returned, and that war-thoughts
	Have left their places vacant, in their rooms
	Come thronging soft and delicate desires,
	All prompting me how fair young Hero is,
	Saying I liked her ere I went to wars.	260

DON PEDRO Thou wilt be like a lover presently,
And tire the hearer with a book of words.
If thou dost love fair Hero, cherish it;
And I will break with her and with her father
And thou shalt have her. Was't not to this end   265
That thou began'st to twist so fine a story?

CLAUDIO How sweetly you do minister to love,
That know love's grief by his complexion!
But lest my liking might too sudden seem,
I would have salved it with a longer treatise.   270

DON PEDRO What need the bridge much broader than the flood?
The fairest grant is the necessity.
Look what will serve is fit. 'Tis once, thou lovest,
And I will fit thee with the remedy.
I know we shall have revelling tonight: 275
I will assume thy part in some disguise,
And tell fair Hero I am Claudio,
And in her bosom I'll unclasp my heart,
And take her hearing prisoner with the force
And strong encounter of my amorous tale.   280
Then after, to her father will I break:
And the conclusion is, she shall be thine.
In practice let us put it presently.

Exeunt.

Renaissance Theatre Company, 1988

RSC, 1976

RSC, 1990

RSC, 2002

In this scene ...

- Leonato's brother Antonio hurries in with a false report: his servant has told him that Don Pedro is in love with Hero.
- Leonato is pleased to hear this but suggests that they wait to see what happens instead of questioning the servant more.

1   **cousin**: kinsman

6   **As ... them**: The outcome will determine if the news is good

7   **Prince**: i.e. Don Pedro

8   **thick-pleached**: closely-intertwined branches / heavily shaded

10   **discovered**: revealed

12   **accordant**: in agreement

12–13   **take ... top**: seize the moment

13–14   **break ... it**: broach the subject with you

15   **wit**: intelligence

18   **appear itself**: actually happens

19   **withal**: with it

20   **peradventure**: perhaps

23   **cry you mercy**: beg your pardon

Think about

- This brief scene introduces the idea of misunderstandings. Why does Leonato think Don Pedro is interested in his daughter?

Outside Leonato's house.

Enter LEONATO, *meeting an old man, his brother,* ANTONIO.

LEONATO	How now, brother! Where is my cousin, your son? Hath he provided this music?
ANTONIO	He is very busy about it. But, brother, I can tell you strange news that you yet dreamt not of.
LEONATO	Are they good?
ANTONIO	As the event stamps them; but they have a good cover, they show well outward. The Prince and Count Claudio, walking in a thick-pleached alley in mine orchard, were thus much overheard by a man of mine: the Prince discovered to Claudio that he loved my niece your daughter, and meant to acknowledge it this night in a dance; and if he found her accordant, he meant to take the present time by the top and instantly break with you of it.
LEONATO	Hath the fellow any wit that told you this?
ANTONIO	A good sharp fellow. I will send for him, and question him yourself.
LEONATO	No, no. We will hold it as a dream till it appear itself. But I will acquaint my daughter withal, that she may be the better prepared for an answer, if peradventure this be true. Go you and tell her of it.

ATTENDANTS *cross the stage, led by Antonio's* SON, *and accompanied by* BALTHASAR *the musician.*

(*To Antonio's* SON) Cousin, you know what you have to do. (*To the* MUSICIAN) O, I cry you mercy, friend: go you with me, and I will use your skill. (*To Antonio's* SON) Good cousin, have a care this busy time.

Exeunt.

In this scene ...

- Don John talks to Conrade about how unhappy he is about the current reconciliation with his brother, Don Pedro.
- Borachio enters with news of Claudio's intended marriage to Hero.
- Don John immediately starts to think of ways to destroy Claudio's happiness.

In the recent battle Don Pedro's opponent was his half-brother Don John. Now they are reconciled and Don John's companion Conrade advises him to hide his bitterness towards his brother.

1   **What the good-year**: What the devil
1–2   **out of measure**: excessively

3   **breeds**: causes it

7   **sufferance**: endurance

8–9   **born under Saturn**: i.e. of a gloomy or depressed personality
10   **mortifying mischief**: fatal disease

13   **tend on**: attend to
14   **claw**: flatter / accommodate
      humour: mood

16   **stood out**: rebelled

18   **grace**: favour

21   **canker**: wild rose

23   **fashion a carriage**: put on a front

26   **enfranchized**: set free
      clog: heavy block of wood used to tether an animal

---Think about---

- What are the causes of Don John's 'sadness' (line 4)? Think about the circumstances he finds himself in, and about his personality.

Outside Leonato's house.

Enter DON JOHN *the bastard and* CONRADE *his companion.*

CONRADE	What the good-year, my lord! Why are you thus out of measure sad?
DON JOHN	There is no measure in the occasion that breeds; therefore the sadness is without limit.
CONRADE	You should hear reason.
DON JOHN	And when I have heard it, what blessing brings it?
CONRADE	If not a present remedy, at least a patient sufferance.
DON JOHN	I wonder that thou – being, as thou sayest thou art, born under Saturn – goest about to apply a moral medicine to a mortifying mischief. I cannot hide what I am. I must be sad when I have cause, and smile at no man's jests; eat when I have stomach, and wait for no man's leisure; sleep when I am drowsy, and tend on no man's business; laugh when I am merry, and claw no man in his humour.
CONRADE	Yea, but you must not make the full show of this till you may do it without controlment. You have of late stood out against your brother; and he hath ta'en you newly into his grace, where it is impossible you should take true root but by the fair weather that you make yourself. It is needful that you frame the season for your own harvest.
DON JOHN	I had rather be a canker in a hedge than a rose in his grace; and it better fits my blood to be disdained of all than to fashion a carriage to rob love from any. In this, though I cannot be said to be a flattering honest man, it must not be denied but I am a plain-dealing villain. I am trusted with a muzzle and enfranchized with a clog: therefore I have decreed not to sing in my cage. If I had my mouth, I would bite; if I had my liberty, I would do my liking. In the meantime, let me be that I am, and seek not to alter me.
CONRADE	Can you make no use of your discontent?

Line numbers: 5, 10, 15, 20, 25, 30

Don John's other companion Borachio enters and tells them that Claudio is intending to marry Hero. Don John holds a grudge against Claudio because of the recent battle.

38 **betroths ... unquietness**: engages himself to noise (which is inevitable in marriage)
39 **Marry**: by the Virgin Mary

42 **proper squire**: handsome fellow (used scornfully here)

45 **forward**: precocious
    March-chick: a chick which has hatched prematurely
46 **entertained for**: hired as
    smoking: i.e. airing the room by burning something strong-smelling

49 **arras**: tapestry wall-hanging

53 **start-up**: upstart
54 **cross**: obstruct
55 **sure**: loyal

58 **were ... mind**: thought like me (i.e. and would poison their food)
59 **prove**: see / discover

Think about

- Look at Don John's expressions of contempt for Claudio in lines 40 and 42. Why might he want to destroy Claudio's happiness? Think of two reasons.

DON JOHN   I make all use of it, for I use it only. Who comes here?

Enter BORACHIO.

What news, Borachio?

BORACHIO   I came yonder from a great supper. The Prince your
brother is royally entertained by Leonato; and I can give   **35**
you intelligence of an intended marriage.

DON JOHN   Will it serve for any model to build mischief on? What
is he for a fool that betroths himself to unquietness?

BORACHIO   Marry, it is your brother's right hand.

DON JOHN   Who? The most exquisite Claudio?   **40**

BORACHIO   Even he.

DON JOHN   A proper squire! And who, and who? Which way looks
he?

BORACHIO   Marry, on Hero, the daughter and heir of Leonato.

DON JOHN   A very forward March-chick! How came you to this?   **45**

BORACHIO   Being entertained for a perfumer, as I was smoking a
musty room, comes me the Prince and Claudio, hand in
hand, in sad conference. I whipped me behind the
arras, and there heard it agreed upon that the Prince
should woo Hero for himself, and having obtained her,   **50**
give her to Count Claudio.

DON JOHN   Come, come, let us thither. This may prove food to my
displeasure. That young start-up hath all the glory of my
overthrow. If I can cross him any way, I bless myself
every way. You are both sure, and will assist me?   **55**

CONRADE   To the death, my lord.

DON JOHN   Let us to the great supper. Their cheer is the greater that
I am subdued. Would the cook were o' my mind! Shall
we go prove what's to be done?

BORACHIO   We'll wait upon your lordship.   **60**

Exeunt.

In this scene ...

- Leonato advises his daughter on how to respond to a proposal from Don Pedro.
- The men enter for a masquerade dance.
- Don John tries to spoil things between Claudio and Hero, telling him that Don Pedro has won Hero for himself.
- Don Pedro explains that this is untrue. He has arranged with Leonato for Hero to marry Claudio.
- Don Pedro plans how to bring Beatrice and Benedick together.

Beatrice says that she is happy to be single but keeps mentioning Benedick and marriage in her conversation.

3 **tartly**: sourly

8 **image**: picture / statue
8–9 **my ... son**: a spoiled child

15 **'a**: he

17 **shrewd**: sharp

18 **curst**: bad-tempered

19–21 **Too curst ... none**: i.e. there will be one less cuckold if I don't get a husband (refers to the Elizabethan joke that the husband of an unfaithful wife grew horns)
23 **Just**: exactly
24 **at Him**: praying to God

26 **the woollen**: rough woollen blankets

Think about

- What is there in Beatrice's conversation that gives away how she really feels about Benedick?

Inside Leonato's house.

Enter LEONATO, ANTONIO, HERO, BEATRICE, MARGARET *and* URSULA.

LEONATO	Was not Count John here at supper?
ANTONIO	I saw him not.
BEATRICE	How tartly that gentleman looks! I never can see him but I am heart-burned an hour after.
HERO	He is of a very melancholy disposition.
BEATRICE	He were an excellent man that were made just in the midway between him and Benedick: the one is too like an image and says nothing, and the other too like my lady's eldest son, evermore tattling.
LEONATO	Then half Signior Benedick's tongue in Count John's mouth, and half Count John's melancholy in Signior Benedick's face –
BEATRICE	With a good leg and a good foot, uncle, and money enough in his purse, such a man would win any woman in the world, if 'a could get her good will.
LEONATO	By my troth, niece, thou wilt never get thee a husband if thou be so shrewd of thy tongue.
ANTONIO	In faith, she's too curst.
BEATRICE	Too curst is more than curst. I shall lessen God's sending that way: for it is said, 'God sends a curst cow short horns', but to a cow too curst he sends none.
LEONATO	So, by being too curst, God will send you no horns.
BEATRICE	Just, if he send me no husband – for the which blessing I am at Him upon my knees every morning and evening. Lord, I could not endure a husband with a beard on his face! I had rather lie in the woollen.
LEONATO	You may light on a husband that hath no beard.

5

10

15

20

25

Beatrice continues to claim that she will never get married. She advises Hero to marry someone that she likes, not just someone who will please her father.

33   **even**: simply
     in earnest: in advance payment
34   **bear-ward**: bear-trainer
     lead ... hell: according to proverb, the fate of unmarried women

41   **bachelors**: this term also applied to women

51   **metal**: substance

54   **marl**: clay
54–5 **Adam's sons**: i.e. all men
55–6 **match ... kindred**: marry a close relative

58   **in that kind**: i.e. propose marriage

Think about

- In lines 45 to 48, what view does Beatrice express about Hero's duty?

- Two statements are made to Hero (in lines 43 to 44 and 57 to 59) but she offers no reply. What do the two statements have in common?

- What does Hero's silence suggest about her?

BEATRICE	What should I do with him? Dress him in my apparel and make him my waiting-gentlewoman? He that hath a beard is more than a youth, and he that hath no beard ₃₀ is less than a man; and he that is more than a youth is not for me, and he that is less than a man, I am not for him. Therefore I will even take sixpence in earnest of the bear-ward, and lead his apes into hell.
LEONATO	Well then, go you into hell? 35
BEATRICE	No, but to the gate – and there will the devil meet me, like an old cuckold with horns on his head, and say, 'Get you to heaven, Beatrice, get you to heaven: here's no place for you maids.' So deliver I up my apes and away to Saint Peter for the heavens. He shows me where 40 the bachelors sit, and there live we as merry as the day is long.
ANTONIO	(*To* HERO) Well, niece, I trust you will be ruled by your father.
BEATRICE	Yes, faith: it is my cousin's duty to make curtsey and say, 45 'Father, as it please you'. But yet for all that, cousin, let him be a handsome fellow – or else make another curtsey and say, 'Father, as it please *me*'.
LEONATO	Well, niece, I hope to see *you* one day fitted with a husband. 50
BEATRICE	Not till God make men of some other metal than earth. Would it not grieve a woman to be over-mastered with a piece of valiant dust? To make an account of her life to a clod of wayward marl? No, uncle, I'll none. Adam's sons are my brethren, and, truly, I hold it a sin to match 55 in my kindred.
LEONATO	(*To* HERO) Daughter, remember what I told you. If the Prince do solicit you in that kind, you know your answer.

Leonato's family believe that Don Pedro is going to try to win Hero. All the men enter in masks for the dance. Don Pedro begins to charm Hero.

61 in good time: 1 soon; 2 in time with the music (i.e. properly)
important: pushy
62 measure: moderation, but also a stately dance
64 cinquepace: lively dance

67 state and ancientry: stately tradition

70 Cousin: all-purpose term for relative
passing: very

73 walk a bout: walk a while / dance
74 So: If

---Think about---

• What views does Beatrice express about marriage in lines 60 to 69?

• Why do you think the women might not be made to wear masks?

• What does Hero's conversation with Don Pedro reveal about her?

79 favour: face
defend: forbid
80 case: i.e. his mask

81 visor: mask
Philemon ... Jove: Philemon, a peasant in a thatched cottage, welcomed Jove, the king of the gods, unaware of his identity.

BEATRICE	The fault will be in the music, cousin, if you be not 60 wooed in good time. If the Prince be too important, tell him there is measure in everything and so dance out the answer. For hear me, Hero: wooing, wedding, and repenting is as a Scotch jig, a measure, and a cinquepace. The first suit is hot and hasty, like a Scotch jig, and full as 65 fantastical; the wedding, mannerly-modest, as a measure, full of state and ancientry; and then comes repentance and, with his bad legs, falls into the cinquepace faster and faster, till he sink into his grave.
LEONATO	Cousin, you apprehend passing shrewdly. 70
BEATRICE	I have a good eye, uncle. I can see a church by daylight.
LEONATO	The revellers are entering, brother. Make good room.

ANTONIO *and* LEONATO *put on their masks.*

Enter DON PEDRO, CLAUDIO, BENEDICK, BALTHASAR, DON JOHN, BORACHIO *and others, in masks, with a drum. A slow dance begins.*

DON PEDRO	Lady, will you walk a bout with your friend?
HERO	So you walk softly, and look sweetly, and say nothing, I am yours for the walk; and especially when I walk away. 75
DON PEDRO	With me in your company?
HERO	I may say so, when I please.
DON PEDRO	And when please you to say so?
HERO	When I like your favour – for God defend the lute should be like the case! 80
DON PEDRO	My visor is Philemon's roof: within the house is Jove.
HERO	Why then your visor should be thatched.
DON PEDRO	Speak low, if you speak love.

They move aside in the dance.

BALTHASAR	Well, I would you did like me.
MARGARET	So would not I, for your own sake. For I have many ill 85 qualities.

Some of the men playfully
pretend that they are not who
they are. Whilst dancing with
Benedick, Beatrice is irritated by
the things her dancing partner
says to her.

93 **clerk**: church official who leads the
responses during services

98 **counterfeit**: imitate

100 **dry hand**: a sign of old age
up and down: exactly

104 **mum**: silence

---Think about

• This scene involves not only
speech, but music and
dance. If you were directing
it, how would you ensure
that each pair of actors
could be heard while the
dance was carrying on?

111 **Hundred Merry Tales**: a joke book

BALTHASAR	Which is one?
MARGARET	I say my prayers aloud.
BALTHASAR	I love you the better: the hearers may cry 'Amen'.
MARGARET	God match me with a good dancer! 90
BALTHASAR	Amen.
MARGARET	And God keep him out of my sight when the dance is done! Answer, clerk.
BALTHASAR	No more words; the clerk is answered.

They move aside in the dance.

URSULA	I know you well enough: you are Signior Antonio. 95
ANTONIO	At a word, I am not.
URSULA	I know you by the waggling of your head.
ANTONIO	To tell you true, I counterfeit him.
URSULA	You could never do him so ill-well unless you were the very man. Here's his dry hand up and down. You are he, 100 you are he.
ANTONIO	At a word, I am not.
URSULA	Come, come, do you think I do not know you by your excellent wit? Can virtue hide itself? Go to, mum, you are he. Graces will appear, and there's an end. 105

They move aside in the dance.

BEATRICE	Will you not tell me who told you so?
BENEDICK	No, you shall pardon me.
BEATRICE	Nor will you not tell me who you are?
BENEDICK	Not now.
BEATRICE	That I was disdainful, and that I had my good wit out of 110 the 'Hundred Merry Tales' – well, this was Signior Benedick that said so.
BENEDICK	What's he?
BEATRICE	I am sure you know him well enough.

In their contest of wits, Beatrice gets the better of Benedick. As the dancers leave, Don John approaches Claudio and spitefully informs him that Don Pedro wants to win Hero for himself.

118–9 Only his gift: His only skill

120 libertines: scoundrels

121 villainy: rudeness

123 fleet: company

would: wish

boarded me: forced his way onto my ship

125 break a comparison: crack a joke

126 peradventure: perhaps

127–8 partridge wing: tiny bit of food

129 leaders: i.e. of the dance

132 turning: dance-step

133 amorous on: in love with

134 withdrawn: called aside

135 visor: masked person

141 birth: high rank

Think about

- Do you think that Beatrice knows that she is talking to Benedick?

- Why does Claudio instantly pretend to be Benedick at line 138?

BENEDICK	Not I, believe me.	**115**
BEATRICE	Did he never make you laugh?	
BENEDICK	I pray you, what is he?	
BEATRICE	Why, he is the Prince's jester, a very dull fool. Only his gift is in devising impossible slanders. None but libertines delight in him, and the commendation is not **120** in his wit, but in his villainy: for he both pleases men and angers them, and then they laugh at him and beat him. I am sure he is in the fleet. I would he had boarded me.	
BENEDICK	When I know the gentleman, I'll tell him what you say.	
BEATRICE	Do, do. He'll but break a comparison or two on me, **125** which, peradventure not marked or not laughed at, strikes him into melancholy. And then there's a partridge wing saved, for the fool will eat no supper that night.	

Music for the dance continues.

	We must follow the leaders.	
BENEDICK	In every good thing.	**130**
BEATRICE	Nay, if they lead to any ill, I will leave them at the next turning.	

Dance continues and ends.

All exit, except DON JOHN, BORACHIO, *and* CLAUDIO.

DON JOHN	Sure my brother is amorous on Hero, and hath withdrawn her father to break with him about it. The ladies follow her and but one visor remains.	**135**
BORACHIO	And that is Claudio. I know him by his bearing.	
DON JOHN	Are not you Signior Benedick?	
CLAUDIO	You know me well: I am he.	
DON JOHN	Signior, you are very near my brother in his love. He is enamoured on Hero. I pray you dissuade him from her. **140** She is no equal for his birth. You may do the part of an honest man in it.	
CLAUDIO	How know you he loves her?	

Claudio is devastated because he thinks that Don Pedro has betrayed his trust and won Hero for himself. Benedick talks to Claudio about it.

151 **save**: except
     office: business

155 **faith**: loyalty
     blood: passion
156 **accident ... proof**: common occurrence
157 **mistrusted not**: i.e. still didn't suspect

162 **willow**: symbol of unrequited love
163 **County**: Count
164 **usurer**: moneylender
     chain: necklace, a symbol of wealth or status

168 **drover**: cattle-dealer

Think about

- What does Claudio's speech (lines 147 to 157) suggest about his attitude to love?

- Does Don John believe that Don Pedro is in love with Hero or is he simply trying to make trouble? Look at the conversation from line 133 to 146.

172–3 **strike ... post**: i.e. hit out at the wrong target

DON JOHN	I heard him swear his affection.	
BORACHIO	So did I too, and he swore he would marry her tonight.	145
DON JOHN	Come, let us to the banquet.	

Exit DON JOHN, *with* BORACHIO.

CLAUDIO	Thus answer I in name of Benedick,	
	But hear these ill news with the ears of Claudio.	
	'Tis certain so: the Prince woos for himself.	
	Friendship is constant in all other things	150
	Save in the office and affairs of love.	
	Therefore all hearts in love use their own tongues.	
	Let every eye negotiate for itself,	
	And trust no agent. For beauty is a witch	
	Against whose charms faith melteth into blood.	155
	This is an accident of hourly proof,	
	Which I mistrusted not. Farewell therefore, Hero!	

Enter BENEDICK.

BENEDICK	Count Claudio?	
CLAUDIO	Yea, the same.	
BENEDICK	Come, will you go with me?	160
CLAUDIO	Whither?	
BENEDICK	Even to the next willow, about your own business, County. What fashion will you wear the garland of? About your neck, like an usurer's chain? Or under your arm, like a lieutenant's scarf? You must wear it one way, for the Prince hath got your Hero.	165
CLAUDIO	I wish him joy of her.	
BENEDICK	Why, that's spoken like an honest drover: so they sell bullocks. But did you think the Prince would have served you thus?	170
CLAUDIO	I pray you, leave me.	
BENEDICK	Ho! Now you strike like the blind man. 'Twas the boy that stole your meat, and you'll beat the post.	

Benedick is angry because Beatrice has ridiculed him. Don Pedro enters and Benedick, believing that Don Pedro won Hero for himself, tells him that Claudio is heartbroken.

175 **creep ... sedges**: i.e. hide

180–1 **puts ... person**: assumes that everyone thinks as she does

181 **gives me out**: gives that report of me

185 **Lady Fame**: Rumour

186 **lodge ... warren**: a lonely hut in a hunting park

190 **forsaken**: abandoned

193 **flat transgression**: simple offence

196 **a trust**: i.e. trusting another person

200 **bestowed**: used

204 **If ... saying**: If they match what you say

Think about

• What has Benedick got wrong in lines 185 to 201?

• If you were a director, how would you ask Benedick to respond to Don Pedro? Should he disapprove, for example?

Claudio	If it will not be, I'll leave *you*.

Exit.

Benedick	Alas, poor hurt fowl, now will he creep into sedges! But 175 that my Lady Beatrice should know me, and not know me! The Prince's fool! Ha! It may be I go under that title because I am merry. Yea, but so I am apt to do myself wrong. I am not so reputed: it is the base, though bitter, disposition of Beatrice that puts the world into her 180 person, and so gives me out. Well, I'll be revenged as I may.

Enter Don Pedro, *with* Leonato *and* Hero *following.*

Don Pedro	(*To* Benedick) Now signior, where's the Count? Did you see him?
Benedick	Troth, my lord, I have played the part of Lady Fame. 185 I found him here as melancholy as a lodge in a warren. I told him, and I think I told him true, that your Grace had got the good will of this young lady; and I offered him my company to a willow-tree, either to make him a garland, as being forsaken, or to bind him up a rod, as 190 being worthy to be whipped.
Don Pedro	To be whipped! What's his fault?
Benedick	The flat transgression of a schoolboy – who being overjoyed with finding a bird's nest, shows it his companion, and he steals it. 195
Don Pedro	Wilt thou make a trust a transgression? The transgression is in the stealer.
Benedick	Yet it had not been amiss the rod had been made, and the garland too: for the garland he might have worn himself, and the rod he might have bestowed on you, 200 who, as I take it, have stolen his bird's nest.
Don Pedro	I will but teach them to sing, and restore them to the owner.
Benedick	If their singing answer your saying, by my faith you say honestly. 205

Benedick loudly complains
about Beatrice's abuse of him.
When she re-enters with
Claudio, he begs Don Pedro for
an excuse to leave.

206 to: with

209 misused: abused
210 but with: with only
211 visor: mask
213–4 a great thaw: i.e. the roads would be
too muddy to allow travel
215 conveyance: skill
mark: target
216 poniards: daggers

218 terminations: sharp words / opinions
220 though: even if
220–1 all … transgressed: i.e. the Garden of
Eden, which Adam and Eve's sin cost
them
222 turned spit: turned the roasting spit
cleft: split for firewood
224 Até: goddess of discord
good apparel: fine clothes
225 scholar: i.e. someone who knows Latin
conjure her: drive her away (like
exorcising a ghost or evil spirit)
227 sanctuary: place of refuge

Think about

• Look at the images in lines
209 to 229. What do they
reveal about the way
Benedick feels about
Beatrice's treatment of him?

• If you were a director, what
would you have Beatrice
doing during lines 231 to
239?

233 Antipodes: opposite side of the world

235 Prester John: legendary Christian king
in Africa or Asia
236 Cham: emperor of China
embassage: mission / errand
238 harpy: a monster with a lion's body,
eagle's talons and wings, and a
woman's beautiful face

DON PEDRO	The Lady Beatrice hath a quarrel to you: the gentleman that danced with her told her she is much wronged by you.
BENEDICK	O, she misused me past the endurance of a block! An oak but with one green leaf on it would have answered 210 her. My very visor began to assume life and scold with her. She told me, not thinking I had been myself, that I was the Prince's jester, that I was duller than a great thaw – huddling jest upon jest with such impossible conveyance upon me that I stood like a man at a mark, 215 with a whole army shooting at me. She speaks poniards, and every word stabs. If her breath were as terrible as her terminations, there were no living near her: she would infect to the north star. I would not marry her, though she were endowed with all that Adam had left 220 him before he transgressed. She would have made Hercules have turned spit, yea, and have cleft his club to make the fire too. Come, talk not of her. You shall find her the infernal Até in good apparel. I would to God some scholar would conjure her. For certainly, while 225 she is here, a man may live as quiet in hell as in a sanctuary, and people sin upon purpose because they would go thither. So indeed, all disquiet, horror, and perturbation follows her.

Enter CLAUDIO *and* BEATRICE.

DON PEDRO	Look, here she comes.	230
BENEDICK	Will your Grace command me any service to the world's end? I will go on the slightest errand now to the Antipodes that you can devise to send me on. I will fetch you a tooth-picker now from the furthest inch of Asia; bring you the length of Prester John's foot; fetch 235 you a hair off the great Cham's beard; do you any embassage to the Pigmies – rather than hold three words' conference with this harpy. You have no employment for me?	
DON PEDRO	None, but to desire your good company.	240

Beatrice hints that Benedick has broken her heart once before. She brings Claudio forward and Don Pedro explains that he has, in fact, won Hero for Claudio.

246 use: interest (monetary)

250–1 So I ... fools: i.e. I don't want Benedick to have sex with me as I would give birth to fools like him.

258 civil: polite
civil ... orange: civil sounds like Seville
259 complexion: Seville oranges were yellow, the colour of jealousy.
260 blazon: description
261 conceit: idea

266 all grace: the grace of God

269 were: would be

Think about

• What do lines 245 to 248 suggest about Beatrice and Benedick's former relationship?

BENEDICK	O God, sir, here's a dish I love not. I cannot endure my Lady Tongue.

Exit BENEDICK.

DON PEDRO	Come, lady, come. You have lost the heart of Signior Benedick.
BEATRICE	Indeed, my lord, he lent it me awhile, and I gave him 245 use for it, a double heart for his single one. Marry, once before he won it of me with false dice: therefore your Grace may well say I have lost it.
DON PEDRO	You have put him down, lady, you have put him down.
BEATRICE	So I would not he should do me, my lord, lest I should 250 prove the mother of fools. I have brought Count Claudio, whom you sent me to seek.
DON PEDRO	Why, how now, Count! Wherefore are you sad?
CLAUDIO	Not sad, my lord.
DON PEDRO	How then? Sick? 255
CLAUDIO	Neither, my lord.
BEATRICE	The Count is neither sad, nor sick, nor merry, nor well; but civil count, civil as an orange, and something of that jealous complexion.
DON PEDRO	I' faith, lady, I think your blazon to be true; though, I'll 260 be sworn, if he be so, his conceit is false. Here, Claudio, I have wooed in thy name, and fair Hero is won. I have broke with her father, and his good will obtained. Name the day of marriage, and God give thee joy!
LEONATO	Count, take of me my daughter, and with her my 265 fortunes. His Grace hath made the match and all grace say Amen to it!
BEATRICE	Speak, Count, 'tis your cue.
CLAUDIO	Silence is the perfectest herald of joy. I were but little happy, if I could say how much. Lady, as you are mine, 270 I am yours: I give away myself for you and dote upon the exchange.

Beatrice jokingly complains that everyone in the world will get married except her. Don Pedro offers to marry her, but she politely refuses.

276 **poor fool**: a term of endearment

276–7 **windy ... care**: safe (windward) side of sorrow

277 **in his ear**: the words give a stage direction for Hero

280 **Good ... alliance**: Thank the lord for marriage

280–1 **Thus ... world**: i.e. everyone gets married

281 **sunburnt**: unattractive

284 **getting**: offspring

291 **no matter**: nothing serious

293 **becomes**: suits

Think about

In the 1993 Branagh film, Don Pedro's proposal is sincere and Beatrice gently refuses.

• How serious do you think Don Pedro's proposal is? What do you think about Beatrice's response?

• In what different ways could you stage this moment?

299 **cry you mercy**: beg your pardon

BEATRICE	Speak, cousin – or, if you cannot, stop his mouth with a kiss, and let not him speak neither.
DON PEDRO	In faith, lady, you have a merry heart.
BEATRICE	Yea, my lord; I thank it, poor fool, it keeps on the windy side of care. My cousin tells him in his ear that he is in her heart.
CLAUDIO	And so she doth, cousin.
BEATRICE	Good Lord, for alliance! Thus goes everyone to the world but I, and I am sunburnt. I may sit in a corner and cry 'Heigh-ho for a husband!'
DON PEDRO	Lady Beatrice, I will get you one.
BEATRICE	I would rather have one of your father's getting. Hath your Grace ne'er a brother like you? Your father got excellent husbands, if a maid could come by them.
DON PEDRO	Will you have *me*, lady?
BEATRICE	No, my lord, unless I might have another for working-days. Your Grace is too costly to wear every day. But I beseech your Grace, pardon me: I was born to speak all mirth and no matter.
DON PEDRO	Your silence most offends me, and to be merry best becomes you; for, out of question, you were born in a merry hour.
BEATRICE	No, sure, my lord, my mother cried. But then there was a star danced, and under that was I born. Cousins, God give you joy!
LEONATO	Niece, will you look to those things I told you of?
BEATRICE	I cry you mercy, uncle. (*To* DON PEDRO) By your Grace's pardon.

Exit BEATRICE.

DON PEDRO	By my troth, a pleasant-spirited lady.

275

280

285

290

295

300

63

Don Pedro suggests that
Beatrice would be an excellent
wife for Benedick and
immediately gets the support of
Hero, Leonato and Claudio.

303   **sad**: 1 sad; 2 serious
      ever: always

307   **out of suit**: out of wooing her

312   **Time ... crutches**: Time will drag
312–3 **till ... rites**: until the marriage is
      consummated
314   **just**: exact

316   **answer my mind**: suit my wishes

317   **breathing**: delay

319   **interim**: meantime

322   **fain**: like to / gladly
323   **minister**: give

325–6 **watchings**: staying awake

329   **modest**: proper / suitable
      office: service

Think about

• How well would Beatrice
  and Benedick be suited as
  husband and wife? Think
  about what qualities they
  have in common and what
  the differences between
  them are.

LEONATO	There's little of the melancholy element in her, my lord. She is never sad but when she sleeps, and not ever sad then: for I have heard my daughter say, she hath often dreamt of unhappiness and waked herself with laughing. 305
DON PEDRO	She cannot endure to hear tell of a husband.
LEONATO	O, by no means. She mocks all her wooers out of suit.
DON PEDRO	She were an excellent wife for Benedick.
LEONATO	O Lord, my lord, if they were but a week married, they would talk themselves mad. 310
DON PEDRO	Count Claudio, when mean you to go to church?
CLAUDIO	Tomorrow, my lord. Time goes on crutches till love have all his rites.
LEONATO	Not till Monday, my dear son, which is hence a just seven-night – and a time too brief, too, to have all things 315 answer my mind.
DON PEDRO	Come, you shake the head at so long a breathing – but I warrant thee, Claudio, the time shall not go dully by us. I will in the interim undertake one of Hercules' labours – which is, to bring Signior Benedick and the 320 Lady Beatrice into a mountain of affection, the one with the other. I would fain have it a match; and I doubt not but to fashion it, if you three will but minister such assistance as I shall give you direction.
LEONATO	My lord, I am for you, though it cost me ten nights' 325 watchings.
CLAUDIO	And I, my lord.
DON PEDRO	And you too, gentle Hero?
HERO	I will do any modest office, my lord, to help my cousin to a good husband. 330

Don Pedro introduces his plan to make Beatrice and Benedick fall in love.

332   strain: family

336   practise on: deceive
337   queasy stomach: distaste / squeamishness (for marriage)

Think about

• What do you know about Don Pedro so far? Think about his attitude to others and their attitudes to him.

• In this scene, Don John's plan to spoil the relationship between Claudio and Hero has been frustrated. Predict what Don John will do now.

DON PEDRO And Benedick is not the unhopefullest husband that I
know. Thus far can I praise him: he is of a noble strain,
of approved valour and confirmed honesty. I will teach
you how to humour your cousin, that she shall fall in
love with Benedick. And I, with your two helps, will so 335
practise on Benedick that, in despite of his quick wit
and his queasy stomach, he shall fall in love with
Beatrice. If we can do this, Cupid is no longer an
archer: his glory shall be ours, for we are the only love-
gods. Go in with me, and I will tell you my drift. 340

Exeunt.

National Theatre, 1981

RSC, 1990

RSC, 2002

RSC, 1996

In this scene ...

- Borachio suggests to Don John that they could convince Claudio that Hero has been unfaithful.
- Don John welcomes this plan and offers to pay Borachio for his part in it.

Don John is furious that his plan to spoil Claudio and Hero's engagement has failed. Borachio suggests another way to prevent the marriage.

3 **cross**: block / obstruct

5 **medicinable**: healing
6 **comes ... affection**: gets in the way of his desires
6–7 **ranges ... mine**: pleases me

15 **instant**: moment

---**Think about**---

- Why does Borachio suggest this plot? What does his suggesting it tell you about Don John as a villain?

- The 1993 Branagh film has Don John creeping away from the party. Other productions have him and Borachio lurking and overhearing the wedding plans in Act 2 Scene 1. Where would you set this scene in a film version?

18 **temper**: mix

20 **marrying**: arranging the marriage of
21 **estimation**: worth
22 **stale**: prostitute

24 **misuse**: mislead / delude
    vex: torment
25 **undo**: ruin

27 **despite**: hurt

Outside Leonato's house.

Enter Don John *and* Borachio.

Don John	It is so: the Count Claudio shall marry the daughter of Leonato.
Borachio	Yea, my lord, but I can cross it.
Don John	Any bar, any cross, any impediment will be medicinable to me. I am sick in displeasure to him, and whatsoever comes athwart his affection ranges evenly with mine. How canst thou cross this marriage?
Borachio	Not honestly, my lord, but so covertly that no dishonesty shall appear in me.
Don John	Show me briefly how.
Borachio	I think I told your lordship a year since how much I am in the favour of Margaret, the waiting-gentlewoman to Hero.
Don John	I remember.
Borachio	I can, at any unseasonable instant of the night, appoint her to look out at her lady's chamber-window.
Don John	What life is in that, to be the death of this marriage?
Borachio	The poison of that lies in you to temper. Go you to the Prince your brother. Spare not to tell him that he hath wronged his honour in marrying the renowned Claudio – whose estimation do you mightily hold up – to a contaminated stale, such a one as Hero.
Don John	What proof shall I make of that?
Borachio	Proof enough to misuse the Prince, to vex Claudio, to undo Hero and kill Leonato. Look you for any other issue?
Don John	Only to despite them I will endeavour anything.

5

10

15

20

25

Borachio outlines his plan to deceive Claudio and Don Pedro into believing that Hero has been unfaithful to Claudio.

28 meet: suitable

30 Intend: Pretend

33 cozened: tricked
semblance ... maid: imitation of a virgin
35 instances: evidence

42 jealousy: suspicion
assurance: certainty

46 ducats: Italian coins

---Think about ---

• List the deceptions that are necessary to make Borachio's plan work. What will Don Pedro, Claudio and Leonato have to believe?

• Why is Conrade absent in this scene, do you think? Think about the differences between Don John's two henchmen.

BORACHIO	Go, then: find me a meet hour to draw Don Pedro and the Count Claudio alone. Tell them that you know that Hero loves me. Intend a kind of zeal both to the Prince 30 and Claudio – as in love of your brother's honour, who hath made this match, and his friend's reputation, who is thus like to be cozened with the semblance of a maid – that you have discovered thus. They will scarcely believe this without trial. Offer them instances, which 35 shall bear no less likelihood than to see me at her chamber window, hear me call Margaret Hero, hear Margaret term me Claudio; and bring them to see this the very night before the intended wedding – for in the meantime I will so fashion the matter that Hero shall be 40 absent – and there shall appear such seeming truth of Hero's disloyalty that jealousy shall be called assurance, and all the preparation overthrown.
DON JOHN	Grow this to what adverse issue it can, I will put it in practice. Be cunning in the working this, and thy fee is 45 a thousand ducats.
BORACHIO	Be you constant in the accusation, and my cunning shall not shame me.
DON JOHN	I will presently go learn their day of marriage.

Exeunt.

In this scene ...

- Benedick cannot understand the way a man alters when he falls in love, as Claudio has.
- Don Pedro, Leonato and Claudio enter, pretending not to see Benedick. Balthasar, one of Don Pedro's men, sings a song.
- To trick Benedick, they loudly discuss Beatrice's love for him.
- Benedick believes the whole story. When the men leave, he decides to return Beatrice's love.

Benedick is complaining about the ways in which being in love has changed Claudio.

5 **I ... already**: i.e. I'll be back instantly

11 **argument**: subject

13–14 **drum ... fife**: soldiers' musical instruments

14–15 **tabor and pipe**: small drum and flute (played in peace time)

17 **carving ... doublet**: designing the style of a new jacket

19–20 **turned orthography**: using flowery language

20 **fantastical**: bizarre

23 **oyster**: a totally silent creature, stuck in its shell

28 **grace**: good graces

Think about

- Benedick describes his ideal woman in lines 28 to 33. How far would Beatrice match his criteria?

- What does Benedick's speech (lines 8 to 21) tell us about the typical behaviour of a lover?

Leonato's garden.

Enter BENEDICK *alone.*

BENEDICK	Boy!

Enter BOY.

BOY	Signior?	
BENEDICK	In my chamber window lies a book: bring it hither to me in the orchard.	
BOY	I am here already, sir.	5
BENEDICK	I know that; but I would have thee hence, and here again.	

Exit BOY.

I do much wonder that one man, seeing how much another man is a fool when he dedicates his behaviours to love, will, after he hath laughed at such shallow 10
follies in others, become the argument of his own scorn by falling in love. And such a man is Claudio. I have known when there was no music with him but the drum and the fife, and now had he rather hear the tabor and the pipe. I have known when he would have walked ten 15
mile afoot to see a good armour, and now will he lie ten nights awake carving the fashion of a new doublet. He was wont to speak plain and to the purpose, like an honest man and a soldier, and now is he turned orthography: his words are a very fantastical banquet, 20
just so many strange dishes. May I be so converted and see with these eyes? I cannot tell: I think not. I will not be sworn but love may transform me to an oyster. But I'll take my oath on it, till he have made an oyster of me, he shall never make me such a fool. One woman is fair, 25
yet I am well; another is wise, yet I am well; another virtuous, yet I am well; but till all graces be in one woman, one woman shall not come in my grace. Rich she shall be, that's certain; wise, or I'll none; virtuous,

As Benedick is imagining his perfect woman, he is interrupted by the entrance of Don Pedro, Leonato and Claudio. As Benedick hides, they pretend not to have noticed him and they urge Balthasar to sing a love song.

Think about

- The expression 'to note' (lines 52 to 55) can mean 'to observe'. What examples have there been so far in the play of people observing something and misinterpreting what they have seen?

- Look at lines 52 to 53. It has been said that the title of this play has several meanings: that it is Much Ado About (a) Not a lot, (b) Noting, and (c) No-thing (a term for a woman's sexual organ). In what ways does the play so far seem to be about (i) mistaking what we think we have 'noted'? and (ii) women, sex and virginity?

30 **cheapen**: bargain for
31 **noble ... angel**: a noble was a coin worth about two-thirds as much as an angel, another coin

40 **fit ... pennyworth**: give Benedick more than he bargained for

42 **tax**: task
43 **slander music**: give music a bad name

44 **witness still**: always a sign
45 **put ... perfection**: play down his own skill
46 **woo**: persuade

54 **crotchets**: 1 musical notes; 2 fanciful ideas

or I'll never cheapen her; fair, or I'll never look on her;   30
mild, or come not near me; noble, or not I for an angel;
of good discourse, an excellent musician, and her hair
shall be – of what colour it please God. Ha! The Prince
and Monsieur Love! I will hide me in the arbour.

He withdraws.

Enter Don Pedro, Leonato, *and* Claudio.

Don Pedro   Come, shall we hear this music?   35

Claudio   Yea, my good lord. How still the evening is,
As hushed on purpose to grace harmony!

Don Pedro   See you where Benedick hath hid himself?

Claudio   O very well, my lord. The music ended,
We'll fit the hid fox with a pennyworth.   40

Enter Balthasar *with musicians.*

Don Pedro   Come, Balthasar, we'll hear that song again.

Balthasar   O, good my lord, tax not so bad a voice
To slander music any more than once.

Don Pedro   It is the witness still of excellency
To put a strange face on his own perfection.   45
I pray thee sing, and let me woo no more.

Balthasar   Because you talk of wooing, I will sing,
Since many a wooer doth commence his suit
To her he thinks not worthy: yet he woos;
Yet will he swear he loves.

Don Pedro   Nay, pray thee, come.   50
Or, if thou wilt hold longer argument,
Do it in notes.

Balthasar   Note this before my notes:
There's not a note of mine that's worth the noting.

Don Pedro   Why, these are very crotchets that he speaks;
Note notes, forsooth, and nothing!   55

Music.

Balthasar sings a song about how men can't be trusted. Benedick, in hiding, complains about the song.

57 **sheep's guts**: i.e. the strings of an instrument
hale: pull

58 **a horn ... money**: I'd rather listen to a hunting horn (another sexual joke)

66 **Hey ... nonny**: i.e. joyful sounds or songs

67 **moe**: more

68 **dumps**: sad moods

69 **fraud**: inconstancy

70 **leavy**: leafy

Think about

- How important are the words of the song? Think about the theme of deception and the difference in the behaviour of men and women.

- The 1993 Branagh film uses the song during the opening titles. What effect does this have on the way we think about the behaviour of the lovers and the things they say about love?

77 **for a shift**: to make do

78 **An**: If

80 **bode**: foretells
had as lief: would rather

81 **night-raven**: an omen of sickness or death

| BENEDICK | (*Aside*) Now, divine air! Now is his soul ravished! Is it not strange that sheep's guts should hale souls out of men's bodies? Well, a horn for my money, when all's done. | |

The Song:

BALTHASAR	Sigh no more, ladies, sigh no more,	
	Men were deceivers ever,	60
	One foot in sea and one on shore,	
	To one thing constant never.	
	Then sigh not so, but let them go,	
	And be you blithe and bonny,	
	Converting all your sounds of woe	65
	Into Hey nonny, nonny.	
	Sing no more ditties, sing no moe,	
	Of dumps so dull and heavy;	
	The fraud of men was ever so,	
	Since summer first was leavy.	70
	Then sigh not so, but let them go,	
	And be you blithe and bonny,	
	Converting all your sounds of woe	
	Into Hey nonny, nonny.	
DON PEDRO	By my troth, a good song.	75
BALTHASAR	And an ill singer, my lord.	
DON PEDRO	Ha, no, no, faith: thou sing'st well enough for a shift.	
BENEDICK	(*Aside*) An he had been a dog that should have howled thus, they would have hanged him. And I pray God his bad voice bode no mischief. I had as lief have heard the night-raven, come what plague could have come after it.	80
DON PEDRO	... Yea, marry, dost thou hear, Balthasar? I pray thee, get us some excellent music; for tomorrow night we would have it at the Lady Hero's chamber window.	
BALTHASAR	The best I can, my lord.	85

To trick Benedick, Leonato, Don Pedro and Claudio discuss Beatrice's love for Benedick, loudly enough for him to overhear.

90 **stalk ... sits**: move quietly, the prey doesn't suspect

92–3 **so dote on**: be so in love with
94 **abhor**: hate

95 **Sits ... corner**: Is that how things stand

97 **enraged**: mad
97–8 **past ... thought**: incredible but true

99 **counterfeit**: pretend

102 **discovers**: reveals

Think about

- Directors sometimes make a joke of the Boy (who Benedick sent on an errand at the beginning of this scene) re-entering while Benedick is trying to hide. Would you do this? If so, when would you have him come in?

- Look at the imagery used in lines 90 and 105 to 106 to describe the entrapment of Benedick. How does it relate to Act 1 Scene 1, line 221?

115 **gull**: trick
116 **Knavery**: i.e. Wicked deceit

DON PEDRO	Do so; farewell.

Exit BALTHASAR.

	Come hither, Leonato. What was it you told me of today, that your niece Beatrice was in love with Signior Benedick?
CLAUDIO	(*Aside*) O, ay; stalk on, stalk on, the fowl sits. (*Aloud*) I 90 did never think that lady would have loved any man.
LEONATO	No, nor I neither; but most wonderful that she should so dote on Signior Benedick, whom she hath in all outward behaviours seemed ever to abhor.
BENEDICK	(*Aside*) Is't possible? Sits the wind in *that* corner? 95
LEONATO	By my troth, my lord, I cannot tell what to think of it: but that she loves him with an enraged affection – it is past the infinite of thought.
DON PEDRO	Maybe she doth but counterfeit.
CLAUDIO	Faith, like enough. 100
LEONATO	O God! Counterfeit? There was never counterfeit of passion came so near the life of passion as she discovers it.
DON PEDRO	Why, what effects of passion shows she?
CLAUDIO	(*To* DON PEDRO *and* LEONATO) Bait the hook well: this 105 fish will bite.
LEONATO	What effects, my lord? She will sit you – you heard my daughter tell you how.
CLAUDIO	She did, indeed.
DON PEDRO	How, how, I pray you? You amaze me. I would have 110 thought her spirit had been invincible against all assaults of affection.
LEONATO	I would have sworn it had, my lord, especially against Benedick.
BENEDICK	(*Aside*) I should think this a gull, but that the white- 115 bearded fellow speaks it. Knavery cannot, sure, hide himself in such reverence.

Don Pedro, Claudio and Leonato describe how desperate Beatrice is because Benedick does not love her back.

119   Hold: Keep

127   smock: undergarment

132   sheet: here also a bed sheet

134   halfpence: tiny bits

136   flout: ridicule

Think about

• Why doesn't Benedick realise that the men aren't telling the truth about Beatrice? What does that suggest about his feelings for her?

142   ecstasy: madness

144   outrage: violence

• If you were the director, how would you stage this scene? Think about what sort of set would be needed.

150   alms: good deed

CLAUDIO	(*To* DON PEDRO *and* LEONATO) He hath ta'en the infection. Hold it up.
DON PEDRO	Hath she made her affection known to Benedick? 120
LEONATO	No, and swears she never will: that's her torment.
CLAUDIO	'Tis true, indeed, so your daughter says. 'Shall I,' says she, 'that have so oft encountered him with scorn, write to him that I love him?'
LEONATO	This says she now when she is beginning to write to 125 him; for she'll be up twenty times a night, and there will she sit in her smock till she have writ a sheet of paper. My daughter tells us all.
CLAUDIO	Now you talk of a sheet of paper, I remember a pretty jest your daughter told us of. 130
LEONATO	O, when she had writ it and was reading it over, she found 'Benedick' and 'Beatrice' between the sheet?
CLAUDIO	That.
LEONATO	O, she tore the letter into a thousand halfpence – railed at herself that she should be so immodest to write to one 135 that she knew would flout her. 'I measure him,' says she, 'by my own spirit; for I should flout him if he writ to me: yea, though I love him, I should.'
CLAUDIO	Then down upon her knees she falls – weeps, sobs, beats her heart, tears her hair, prays, curses – 'O sweet 140 Benedick! God give me patience!'
LEONATO	She doth indeed; my daughter says so. And the ecstasy hath so much overborne her that my daughter is sometime afeard she will do a desperate outrage to herself. It is very true. 145
DON PEDRO	It were good that Benedick knew of it by some other, if she will not discover it.
CLAUDIO	To what end? He would make but a sport of it, and torment the poor lady worse.
DON PEDRO	An he should, it were an alms to hang him. She's an 150 excellent sweet lady, and, out of all suspicion, she is virtuous.

The men express their sympathy for Beatrice and criticism of Benedick if he does not return her love.

155 **blood**: passion
156 **ten ... one**: i.e. the odds are very good

159 **dotage**: adoration
160 **daffed**: put aside
     made ... myself: married her

166 **bate**: lessen
     accustomed: customary

167 **tender**: offer

169 **contemptible**: scoffing

170 **proper**: handsome

171 **hath ... happiness**: i.e. is good-looking enough

175 **Hector**: the most valiant of the Trojan warriors
     quarrels: duels

Think about

• Which of the men's statements about Benedick are true and which are intended to wind him up?

183 **howsoever**: even though
183–4 **some ... make**: the rude jokes he tells

CLAUDIO	And she is exceeding wise.
DON PEDRO	In everything but in loving Benedick.
LEONATO	O, my lord, wisdom and blood combating in so tender 155 a body, we have ten proofs to one that blood hath the victory. I am sorry for her, as I have just cause, being her uncle and her guardian.
DON PEDRO	I would she had bestowed this dotage on me. I would have daffed all other respects and made her half myself. 160 I pray you, tell Benedick of it, and hear what he will say.
LEONATO	Were it good, think you?
CLAUDIO	Hero thinks surely she will die: for she says she will die if he love her not. And she will die ere she make her love known. And she will die, if he woo her, rather than 165 she will bate one breath of her accustomed crossness.
DON PEDRO	She doth well. If she should make tender of her love, 'tis very possible he'll scorn it: for the man, as you know all, hath a contemptible spirit.
CLAUDIO	He is a very proper man. 170
DON PEDRO	He hath, indeed, a good outward happiness.
CLAUDIO	Before God, and in my mind, very wise.
DON PEDRO	He doth, indeed, show some sparks that are like wit.
CLAUDIO	And I take him to be valiant.
DON PEDRO	As Hector, I assure you. And in the managing of quarrels 175 you may say he is wise: for either he avoids them with great discretion, or undertakes them with a most Christian-like fear.
LEONATO	If he do fear God, 'a must necessarily keep peace. If he break the peace, he *ought* to enter into a quarrel with 180 fear and trembling.
DON PEDRO	And so will he do, for the man doth fear God – howsoever it seems not in him by some large jests he will make. Well, I am sorry for your niece. Shall we go seek Benedick, and tell him of her love? 185

The men discuss whether their scheme will be successful. Benedick begins to consider his feelings for Beatrice.

186 **wear it out**: get over it in time

198–9 **they ... dotage**: each one believes that the other is in love with them
199 **no such matter**: that isn't the case
200–1 **dumb-show**: mime

203 **sadly**: seriously
204–5 **have ... bent**: are stretched to the limit
205 **requited**: returned
206 **censured**: criticised

Think about

• Don Pedro imagines that when Beatrice and Benedick meet, these two witty people will not be able to think of a word to say (lines 198 to 201). What do you think will happen when Benedick next meets Beatrice?

• Benedick has an instant change of heart. What does this suggest about his earlier statements about marriage and his earlier criticisms of Beatrice?

210 **detractions**: bad points

213 **reprove**: disprove
214 **argument**: proof

216 **quirks**: jokes

220–1 **Shall ... humour?**: i.e. Should a man be put off what he wants to do by a few cheap jokes and wise sayings?

CLAUDIO	Never tell him, my lord. Let her wear it out with good counsel.
LEONATO	Nay, that's impossible. She may wear her heart out first.
DON PEDRO	Well, we will hear further of it by your daughter: let it cool the while. I love Benedick well. And I could wish 190 he would modestly examine himself, to see how much he is unworthy so good a lady.
LEONATO	My lord, will you walk? Dinner is ready.
CLAUDIO	(*Aside*) If he do not dote on her upon this, I will never trust my expectation. 195
DON PEDRO	(*Aside to* LEONATO) Let there be the same net spread for her; and that must your daughter and her gentlewomen carry. The sport will be, when they hold one an opinion of another's dotage – and no such matter. That's the scene that I would see, which will be merely a dumb- 200 show. Let us send her to call him in to dinner.

Exit DON PEDRO, *with* CLAUDIO *and* LEONATO.

BENEDICK	(*Coming forward*) This can be no trick. The conference was sadly borne. They have the truth of this from Hero. They seem to pity the lady: it seems her affections have their full bent. Love me? Why, it must be requited. I hear 205 how I am censured: they say I will bear myself proudly, if I perceive the love come from her. They say, too, that she will rather die than give any sign of affection. I did never think to marry. I must not seem proud: happy are they that hear their detractions and can put them to 210 mending. They say the lady is fair – 'tis a truth, I can bear them witness; and virtuous – 'tis so, I cannot reprove it; and wise – but for loving me. By my troth, it is no addition to her wit, nor no great argument of her folly – for I will be horribly in love with her. I may 215 chance have some odd quirks and remnants of wit broken on me, because I have railed so long against marriage. But doth not the appetite alter? A man loves the meat in his youth that he cannot endure in his age. Shall quips and sentences and these paper bullets of the 220 brain awe a man from the career of his humour? No: the

Benedick is amazed to discover that he loves Beatrice. She arrives to ask Benedick to come in to dinner and is puzzled by his strange behaviour.

233 daw: jackdaw (thought to be a foolish bird)
withal: with
have no stomach: are obviously not hungry

Think about

- Benedick's statement 'If I do not love her, I am a Jew' (line 240) seems racist. What does Benedick actually mean? Think about the association of Jews in Shakespeare's time with (a) Christ's crucifixion and (b) financial meanness.

- If you were a director, how would you deal with this in a production? Would you cut the line, change it or leave it as it is? Why?

240 Jew: often a term of abuse in Shakespeare's time

world must be peopled. When I said I would die a
bachelor, I did not think I should live till I were married.
Here comes Beatrice. By this day, she's a fair lady! I do
spy some marks of love in her.   225

Enter BEATRICE.

BEATRICE   Against my will I am sent to bid you come in to dinner.

BENEDICK   Fair Beatrice, I thank you for your pains.

BEATRICE   I took no more pains for those thanks than you take
              pains to thank me. If it had been painful I would not
              have come.   230

BENEDICK   You take pleasure then in the message?

BEATRICE   Yea, just so much as you may take upon a knife's point,
              and choke a daw withal. You have no stomach, signior.
              Fare you well.

                                                              Exit.

BENEDICK   Ha! 'Against my will I am sent to bid you come in to 235
              dinner'– there's a double meaning in that. 'I took no
              more pains for those thanks than you took pains to
              thank me'– that's as much as to say, 'Any pains that I
              take for you is as easy as thanks.' If I do not take pity of
              her, I am a villain! If I do not love her, I am a Jew. I will 240
              go get her picture.

                                                              Exit.

RSC, 2002

RSC, 1996

Cheek by Jowl, 1998

Open Air Theatre, Regent's Park, 2000

In this scene ...

- Hero asks Margaret to tell Beatrice that she and Ursula are talking about Beatrice in the garden.
- Ursula and Hero stand near to where Beatrice is hiding and discuss Benedick's love for Beatrice and the fact that she does not return it.
- Beatrice is dismayed to realise how proud and scornful she seems to others.
- Beatrice resolves to return Benedick's love.

Margaret goes to find Beatrice to tell her that Hero and Ursula are in the garden, talking about her. Believing her, Beatrice hides where she can hear their conversation.

3 **Proposing**: talking

7 **pleachèd**: with branches twisted around each other
9 **favourites**: favoured courtiers

11 **power**: i.e. of the princes
12 **propose**: conversation
    office: responsibility

14 **presently**: immediately

16 **trace**: tread

23 **hearsay**: rumour

24 **lapwing**: a bird which stays low to the ground to escape notice

Think about

Hero's speeches offer some details to the set designer:
- What sort of scenery does this scene require on a modern stage?

- Where is Beatrice expected to hide?

Leonato's garden.

Enter HERO *and her two gentlewomen,* MARGARET *and* URSULA.

HERO	Good Margaret, run thee to the parlour.
	There shalt thou find my cousin Beatrice
	Proposing with the Prince and Claudio.
	Whisper her ear, and tell her I and Ursula

Walk in the orchard, and our whole discourse   5
Is all of her. Say that thou overheard'st us,
And bid her steal into the pleachèd bower,
Where honeysuckles, ripened by the sun,
Forbid the sun to enter – like favourites,
Made proud by princes, that advance their pride   10
Against that power that bred it. There will she hide her,
To listen our propose. This is thy office:
Bear thee well in it, and leave us alone.

MARGARET   I'll make her come, I warrant you, presently.

                                        Exit.

HERO   Now Ursula, when Beatrice doth come,   15
As we do trace this alley up and down,
Our talk must only be of Benedick.
When I do name him, let it be thy part
To praise him more than ever man did merit.
My talk to thee must be how Benedick   20
Is sick in love with Beatrice. Of this matter
Is little Cupid's crafty arrow made,
That only wounds by hearsay. Now begin –

Enter BEATRICE, *trying not to be seen: she slips into hiding.*

     – For look where Beatrice like a lapwing runs
Close by the ground, to hear our conference.   25

Ursula and Hero loudly discuss Benedick's love for Beatrice and Beatrice's scorn for men in general.

27 **oars**: fins

30 **couchèd**: hidden
    woodbine coverture: cover of honeysuckle

35 **coy**: stand-offish / distant
36 **haggards**: wild hawks

38 **my ... lord**: my fiancé

42 **wish him**: advise him to

Think about

• Find the animal imagery in lines 24 to 36. How does this compare with the language used about the trapping of Benedick in Act 2 Scene 3?

• In what ways is Hero's condemnation of Beatrice similar to the men's condemnation of Benedick in Act 2 Scene 3?

45 **as full ... bed**: i.e. as happy a marriage
46 **couch**: lie

52 **Misprizing**: undervaluing

54 **All matter else**: i.e. everyone else's wit
55 **take ... affection**: understand the idea of being in love
56 **self-endeared**: in love with herself

URSULA	(*To* HERO) The pleasant'st angling is to see the fish
	Cut with her golden oars the silver stream,
	And greedily devour the treacherous bait.
	So angle we for Beatrice, who even now
	Is couchèd in the woodbine coverture. **30**
	Fear you not my part of the dialogue.
HERO	(*To* URSULA) Then go we near her, that her ear lose
	nothing
	Of the false sweet bait that we lay for it.

They approach BEATRICE's *hiding-place.*

	(*Aloud*) No, truly, Ursula, she is too disdainful.
	I know her spirits are as coy and wild **35**
	As haggards of the rock.
URSULA	But are you sure
	That Benedick loves Beatrice so entirely?
HERO	So says the Prince and my new-trothèd lord.
URSULA	And did they bid you tell her of it, madam?
HERO	They did entreat me to acquaint her of it. **40**
	But I persuaded them, if they loved Benedick,
	To wish him wrestle with affection,
	And never to let Beatrice know of it.
URSULA	Why did you so? Doth not the gentleman
	Deserve as full as fortunate a bed **45**
	As ever Beatrice shall couch upon?
HERO	O god of love! I know he doth deserve
	As much as may be yielded to a man.
	But Nature never framed a woman's heart
	Of prouder stuff than that of Beatrice. **50**
	Disdain and scorn ride sparkling in her eyes,
	Misprizing what they look on, and her wit
	Values itself so highly that to her
	All matter else seems weak. She cannot love,
	Nor take no shape nor project of affection, **55**
	She is so self-endeared.

Hero says that she will advise Benedick to get over his love for Beatrice. Playing along, Ursula suggests that Hero is being too hard on Beatrice.

57 **were not**: would not be

60 **How**: no matter how
    rarely featured: handsome
61 **spell him backward**: turn his virtues into faults
63 **black**: of a dark complexion
    antic: grotesque clown
64 **lance ill-headed**: badly-tipped spear
65 **low**: short
    agate: small ornamental stone, often carved with images of people

70 **simpleness**: sincerity
    purchaseth: deserve
71 **carping**: criticising

72 **odd ... fashions**: over-particular

76 **press ... death**: torture

78 **Consume ... sighs**: referring to the belief that each sigh costs the heart one drop of blood
79 **were**: would be

84 **honest**: harmless

Think about

- What differences are there between the things the men said about Benedick for him to overhear and those that the women say about Beatrice for her to overhear?

- Directors usually try to make this scene different from Act 2 Scene 3. How would you stage it?

URSULA	Sure, I think so;
	And therefore, certainly, it were not good
	She knew his love, lest she'll make sport at it.

HERO	Why, you speak truth. I never yet saw man,	
	How wise, how noble, young, how rarely featured,	60
	But she would spell him backward. If fair-faced,	
	She would swear the gentleman should be her sister;	
	If black, why, Nature, drawing of an antic,	
	Made a foul blot; if tall, a lance ill-headed;	
	If low, an agate very vilely cut;	65
	If speaking, why, a vane blown with all winds;	
	If silent, why, a block movèd with none.	
	So turns she every man the wrong side out,	
	And never gives to truth and virtue that	
	Which simpleness and merit purchaseth.	70

URSULA	Sure, sure, such carping is not commendable.

HERO	No; not to be so odd and from all fashions,	
	As Beatrice is, cannot be commendable.	
	But who dare tell her so? If I should speak,	
	She would mock me into air. O, she would laugh me	75
	Out of myself, press me to death with wit!	
	Therefore let Benedick, like covered fire,	
	Consume away in sighs, waste inwardly.	
	It were a better death than die with mocks,	
	Which is as bad as die with tickling.	80

URSULA	Yet tell her of it: hear what she will say.

HERO	No: rather I will go to Benedick	
	And counsel him to fight against his passion.	
	And, truly, I'll devise some honest slanders	
	To stain my cousin with. One doth not know	85
	How much an ill word may empoison liking.	

URSULA	O, do not do your cousin such a wrong!	
	She cannot be so much without true judgement –	
	Having so swift and excellent a wit	
	As she is prized to have – as to refuse	90
	So rare a gentleman as Signior Benedick.	

When Beatrice is left alone, she declares that she will change her proud ways and return Benedick's love.

Think about

- Lines 35 to 36 and line 112 both say that Beatrice is like a wild bird who will be tamed by Benedick. What is the effect in this scene of the hawk-taming imagery?

- There are several references to Cupid in this scene (look at lines 21 to 23 and 106). How do the characters describe Cupid throughout the play? Is love a matter of chance, or is it arranged by others?

92 **only**: the best

96 **argument**: conversational skill

98 **name**: reputation

101 **every day tomorrow**: i.e. every day of my life, starting tomorrow

102 **attires**: head-dresses

104 **limed**: trapped

105 **haps**: chance

107 **fire ... ears**: referring to the idea that your ears burn when someone talks about you

110 **No ... such**: No-one speaks well of proud people behind their backs

116 **better ... reportingly**: more than by hearsay

HERO	He is the only man of Italy – Always excepted my dear Claudio.
URSULA	I pray you be not angry with me, madam, Speaking my fancy: Signior Benedick, 95 For shape, for bearing, argument and valour, Goes foremost in report through Italy.
HERO	Indeed, he hath an excellent good name.
URSULA	His excellence did earn it ere he had it. When are you married, madam? 100
HERO	Why, every day tomorrow! Come, go in. I'll show thee some attires, and have thy counsel Which is the best to furnish me tomorrow.
URSULA	(*To* HERO) She's limed, I warrant you: we have caught her, madam.
HERO	(*To* URSULA) If it prove so, then loving goes by haps: 105 Some Cupid kills with arrows, some with traps.

Exit HERO, *with* URSULA.

BEATRICE	(*Coming forward*) What fire is in mine ears? Can this be true? Stand I condemned for pride and scorn so much? Contempt, farewell! and maiden pride, adieu! No glory lives behind the back of such. 110 And Benedick, love on. I will requite thee, Taming my wild heart to thy loving hand. If thou dost love, my kindness shall incite thee To bind our loves up in a holy band. For others say thou dost deserve, and I 115 Believe it better than reportingly.

Exit.

RSC, 1986

RSC, 1996

National Theatre, 1981

In this scene ...

• Don Pedro, Claudio and Leonato tease Benedick about how his behaviour and appearance have altered.

• They congratulate one another on the success of their plan to make Benedick fall in love with Beatrice.

• Don John tells Don Pedro and Claudio that he has proof that Hero has been unfaithful to Claudio.

Don Pedro, Claudio and Leonato tease Benedick about his changed behaviour and appearance.

Think about

• In the 1993 Branagh film, Benedick is shown preening himself in front of a mirror. In what other ways could an actor show the change in his behaviour?

• Which qualities of Benedick's is Don Pedro making fun of?

3 **vouchsafe**: allow

6 **only be bold with**: i.e. take only

9 **hangman**: i.e. rascal

14 **sadder**: more serious

17 **wants**: lacks

19 **toothache**: frequently associated with love-sickness
20 **Draw it**: Pull it out
21 **Hang it**: Curse it
22 **hang ... afterwards**: a reference to executions in which the victim was hung, drawn and quartered
24 **Where ... worm**: Toothaches were supposedly caused by imbalances of bodily fluids or by worms.

At Leonato's house.

Enter DON PEDRO, CLAUDIO, BENEDICK *and* LEONATO.

DON PEDRO	I do but stay till your marriage be consummate, and then go I toward Aragon.
CLAUDIO	I'll bring you thither, my lord, if you'll vouchsafe me.
DON PEDRO	Nay, that would be as great a soil in the new gloss of your marriage as to show a child his new coat and forbid him to wear it. I will only be bold with Benedick for his company; for, from the crown of his head to the sole of his foot, he is all mirth. He hath twice or thrice cut Cupid's bow-string and the little hangman dare not shoot at him. He hath a heart as sound as a bell and his tongue is the clapper – for what his heart thinks, his tongue speaks.
BENEDICK	Gallants, I am not as I have been.
LEONATO	So say I: methinks you are sadder.
CLAUDIO	I hope he be in love.
DON PEDRO	Hang him, truant! There's no true drop of blood in him to be truly touched with love. If he be sad, he wants money.
BENEDICK	I have the toothache.
DON PEDRO	Draw it.
BENEDICK	Hang it!
CLAUDIO	You must hang it first, and draw it afterwards.
DON PEDRO	What! Sigh for the toothache?
LEONATO	Where is but a humour or a worm.
BENEDICK	Well, everyone can master a grief but he that has it.
CLAUDIO	Yet say I, he is in love.

5

10

15

20

25

The men try to get Benedick to admit that he is in love.

27–8 **fancy ... fancy**: infatuation ... fad

28 **disguises**: outfits / costumes

31 **slops**: loose breeches

36 **old**: customary
'A: He
o' mornings: every morning

40–1 **old ... tennis-balls**: tennis balls were stuffed with hair in Elizabethan times

44 **civet**: perfume

47 **note**: sign

48 **wont**: accustomed

49 **paint himself**: wear cosmetics

51–2 **lute-string**: lutes were used to play love songs

52 **governed by stops**: regulated by frets (on a lute)

58 **ill conditions**: bad qualities

Think about

- How did Benedick look before and how does he look now? Looking at lines 27 to 37 in particular, think about how his clothes and facial appearance might have changed now that he is in love.

DON PEDRO	There is no appearance of fancy in him, unless it be a fancy that he hath to strange disguises – as to be a Dutchman today, a Frenchman tomorrow, or in the shape of two countries at once, as a German from the 30 waist downward, all slops, and a Spaniard from the hip upward, no doublet. Unless he have a fancy to this foolery, as it appears he hath, he is no fool for fancy, as you would have it appear he is.
CLAUDIO	If he be not in love with some woman, there is no 35 believing old signs. 'A brushes his hat o' mornings: what should that bode?
DON PEDRO	Hath any man seen him at the barber's?
CLAUDIO	No – but the barber's man hath been seen with him, and the old ornament of his cheek hath already stuffed 40 tennis-balls.
LEONATO	Indeed, he looks younger than he did, by the loss of a beard.
DON PEDRO	Nay, 'a rubs himself with civet: can you smell him out by that? 45
CLAUDIO	That's as much as to say, the sweet youth's in love.
DON PEDRO	The greatest note of it is his melancholy.
CLAUDIO	And when was he wont to wash his face?
DON PEDRO	Yea, or to paint himself? For the which, I hear what they say of him. 50
CLAUDIO	Nay, but his jesting spirit, which is now crept into a lute-string, and now governed by stops.
DON PEDRO	Indeed, that tells a heavy tale for him. Conclude, conclude: he is in love.
CLAUDIO	Nay, but I know who loves him. 55
DON PEDRO	That would I know too. I warrant, one that knows him not.
CLAUDIO	Yes, and his ill conditions; and, in despite of all, dies for him.

Benedick takes Leonato aside to speak to him. Don John arrives to see Don Pedro and Claudio. He seems concerned about the marriage between Claudio and Hero.

61   charm: cure

63   hobby-horses: buffoons

65   break: talk

70   e'en: evening

71   If ... served: If you are free

Think about

• 'Dies' (in line 58) also meant 'has an orgasm'. How does Don Pedro's reply (line 60) show that he has picked up the *double-entendre* (double meaning)?

80   discover: reveal

• How do you feel about this exchange? Think about whether you find it funny or crude, for example. How does it affect your impressions of Don Pedro and Claudio?

82   aim better at: think better of
83   manifest: make plain
84   holp: helped

87–8   circumstances shortened: to cut a long story short

DON PEDRO	She shall be buried with her face upwards.	60

BENEDICK   Yet is this no charm for the toothache. (*To* LEONATO) Old signior, walk aside with me. I have studied eight or nine wise words to speak to you, which these hobby-horses must not hear.

> *Exit* BENEDICK, *with* LEONATO.

DON PEDRO	For my life, to break with him about Beatrice.	65

CLAUDIO   'Tis even so. Hero and Margaret have by this played their parts with Beatrice; and then the two bears will not bite one another when they meet.

> *Enter* DON JOHN.

DON JOHN   My lord and brother, God save you!

DON PEDRO	Good-e'en, brother.	70

DON JOHN   If your leisure served, I would speak with you.

DON PEDRO   In private?

DON JOHN   If it please you. Yet Count Claudio may hear, for what I would speak of concerns him.

DON PEDRO	What's the matter?	75

DON JOHN   (*To* CLAUDIO) Means your lordship to be married tomorrow?

DON PEDRO   You know he does.

DON JOHN   I know not that, when he knows what I know.

CLAUDIO	If there be any impediment, I pray you discover it.	80

DON JOHN   (*To* CLAUDIO) You may think I love you not. Let that appear hereafter, and aim better at me by that I now will manifest. For my brother, I think he holds you well, and in dearness of heart hath holp to effect your ensuing marriage – surely suit ill spent, and labour ill bestowed! **85**

DON PEDRO   Why, what's the matter?

DON JOHN   I came hither to tell you – and, circumstances shortened, for she has been too long a talking of, the lady is disloyal.

Don John says that he has proof that Hero has been unfaithful to Claudio. He invites Don Pedro and Claudio to see the evidence that night.

94 paint out: describe

96 Wonder ... warrant: Don't try to puzzle it out until you have seen more proof.

103 confess not: don't admit

108 in the congregation: among the people gathered for the wedding

112 disparage: insult
113 Bear it coldly: Keep calm

115 untowardly turned: turned out for the worst
116 mischief ... thwarting: evil striking unexpectedly

Think about

- Claudio is young and sometimes seems to rely on Don Pedro's judgement rather than on his own (look at Act 1 Scene 1, lines 244 to 282). How does Don John exploit that in this scene?

- Which parts of this scene reinforce the idea that this play is Much Ado About (a) No-thing (see 'Think about' on page 76) and (b) Noting (look at lines 103 to 104)?

CLAUDIO	Who? Hero?	90
DON JOHN	Even she – Leonato's Hero, your Hero: every man's Hero.	
CLAUDIO	Disloyal?	
DON JOHN	The word is too good to paint out her wickedness. I could say she were worse: think you of a worse title, and I will fit her to it. Wonder not till further warrant. Go but with me tonight, you shall see her chamber-window entered, even the night before her wedding-day. If you love her then, tomorrow wed her. But it would better fit your honour to change your mind.	95 100
CLAUDIO	May this be so?	
DON PEDRO	I will not think it.	
DON JOHN	If you dare not trust that you see, confess not that you know. If you will follow me, I will show you enough. And when you have seen more and heard more, proceed accordingly.	105
CLAUDIO	If I see anything tonight why I should not marry her, tomorrow in the congregation, where I should wed, there will I shame her.	
DON PEDRO	And, as I wooed for thee to obtain her, I will join with thee to disgrace her.	110
DON JOHN	I will disparage her no farther till you are my witnesses. Bear it coldly but till midnight, and let the issue show itself.	
DON PEDRO	O day untowardly turned!	115
CLAUDIO	O mischief strangely thwarting!	
DON JOHN	O plague right well prevented! So will you say when you have seen the sequel.	

Exeunt.

In this scene ...

- The bumbling Dogberry and Verges inform the Watch of their duties.
- Borachio brags to Conrade that he has earned money from Don John for dishonouring Hero.
- Despite not being very good at their job, the Watch manage to arrest Borachio and Conrade.

Dogberry and Verges summon the Watch and decide who should be in charge of the night patrol.

s.d. **Watch**: part-time police
 1 **true**: honest
 2 **salvation**: he means 'damnation'

 7 **give ... charge**: describe their duties
 8 **desertless**: he means 'deserving'
 9 **constable**: head of the watch patrol (Dogberry is Master Constable)

13 **well-favoured**: handsome

Think about

- Dogberry is a master of malapropisms (using the wrong word). What examples are there in this scene (lines 1 to 84) of words which mean the opposite of what he intends?

- In a stage production, should the men of the Watch understand Dogberry completely, do you think?

20 **senseless**: he means 'sensible'
22 **comprehend ... vagrom ...**: he means 'apprehend' ... 'vagrant' ...
23 **stand**: stop

24 **'a**: he

110

Near Leonato's house.

Enter DOGBERRY *and his partner* VERGES, *with men of the Watch.*

DOGBERRY	Are you good men and true?
VERGES	Yea, or else it were pity but they should suffer salvation, body and soul.
DOGBERRY	Nay, that were a punishment too good for them, if they should have any allegiance in them, being chosen for 5 the Prince's watch.
VERGES	Well, give them their charge, neighbour Dogberry.
DOGBERRY	First, who think you the most desertless man to be constable?
WATCHMAN 1	Hugh Oatcake, sir, or George Seacoal, for they can 10 write and read.
DOGBERRY	Come hither, neighbour Seacoal. God hath blessed you with a good name. To be a well-favoured man is the gift of fortune; but to write and read comes by nature.
WATCHMAN 2	Both which, Master Constable – 15
DOGBERRY	You have. I knew it would be your answer. Well, for your favour, sir, why, give God thanks, and make no boast of it; and for your writing and reading, let that appear when there is no need of such vanity. You are thought here to be the most senseless and fit man for the constable of the 20 watch: therefore bear you the lantern. This is your charge: you shall comprehend all vagrom men – you are to bid any man stand, in the Prince's name.
WATCHMAN 2	How if 'a will not stand?
DOGBERRY	Why, then, take no note of him, but let him go – and 25 presently call the rest of the watch together and thank God you are rid of a knave.

Dogberry gives the Watch their instructions.

30 meddle: deal

32 tolerable: he means 'intolerable' (cannot be suffered)

34–5 belongs to: is appropriate for

36 ancient: experienced

38 bills: weapons

---Think about---

• Find the word-play in Dogberry's speech (lines 52 to 55). Do you think he intends the pun?

• From what you have seen of Dogberry so far, what sort of actor would you cast in the role if you were the director?

52–3 they ... defiled: i.e. if you associate with bad people you pick up their bad ways
pitch: tar

60 still: quieten

VERGES	If he will not stand when he is bidden, he is none of the Prince's subjects.
DOGBERRY	True, and they are to meddle with none but the Prince's **30** subjects. You shall also make no noise in the streets: for, for the watch to babble and to talk is most tolerable and not to be endured.
WATCHMAN 1	We will rather sleep than talk. We know what belongs to a watch. **35**
DOGBERRY	Why, you speak like an ancient and most quiet watchman, for I cannot see how sleeping should offend – only have a care that your bills be not stolen. Well, you are to call at all the ale-houses, and bid those that are drunk get them to bed. **40**
WATCHMAN 2	How if they will not?
DOGBERRY	Why, then, let them alone till they are sober. If they make you not then the better answer, you may say they are not the men you took them for.
WATCHMAN 2	Well, sir. **45**
DOGBERRY	If you meet a thief, you may suspect him, by virtue of your office, to be no true man. And, for such kind of men, the less you meddle or make with them, why, the more is for your honesty.
WATCHMAN 2	If we know him to be a thief, shall we not lay hands on **50** him?
DOGBERRY	Truly, by your office you may, but I think they that touch pitch will be defiled. The most peaceable way for you, if you *do* take a thief, is to let him show himself what he is and steal out of your company. **55**
VERGES	You have been always called a merciful man, partner.
DOGBERRY	Truly, I would not hang a dog by my will, much more a man who hath any honesty in him.
VERGES	If you hear a child cry in the night, you must call to the nurse and bid her still it. **60**

Dogberry and Verges leave the watchmen to their duties, having asked them to keep an eye on Leonato's house. Conrade and Borachio enter and the watchmen overhear their conversation.

67 **present**: represent
68 **stay**: detain

70 **Five ... on't**: I'll bet five to one

75–6 **An ... chances**: If anything serious happens
76–7 **Keep ... own**: i.e. Be discreet

83 **coil**: fuss
84 **vigitant**: he means 'vigilant'

Think about

- In Shakespeare's time town constables and watchmen were often considered a joke because of their incompetence. What is your impression of the Watch so far?

89 **Mass**: By the Mass (an oath)
90 **scab**: also means 'villain'

WATCHMAN 2	How if the nurse be asleep and will not hear us?
DOGBERRY	Why, then, depart in peace, and let the child wake her with crying: for the ewe that will not hear her lamb when it baas will never answer a calf when he bleats.
VERGES	'Tis very true.
DOGBERRY	This is the end of the charge. You, constable, are to present the Prince's own person. If you meet the Prince in the night, you may stay him.
VERGES	Nay, by'r Lady, that I think 'a cannot.
DOGBERRY	Five shillings to one on't, with any man that knows the statutes: he may stay him. Marry, not without the Prince be willing – for, indeed, the watch ought to offend no man, and it is an offence to stay a man against his will.
VERGES	By'r Lady, I think it be so.
DOGBERRY	Ha, ah ha! Well, masters, good night. An there be any matter of weight chances, call up me. Keep your fellows' counsels and your own, and good night. Come, neighbour.
WATCHMAN 1	Well, masters, we hear our charge. Let us go sit here upon the church-bench till two, and then all to bed.
DOGBERRY	One word more, honest neighbours. I pray you, watch about Signior Leonato's door – for the wedding being there tomorrow, there is a great coil tonight. Adieu: be vigitant, I beseech you.

Exit DOGBERRY, *with* VERGES.

Enter BORACHIO *and* CONRADE.

BORACHIO	What, Conrade!
WATCHMAN 2	(*Aside*) Peace! Stir not.
BORACHIO	Conrade, I say!
CONRADE	Here, man; I am at thy elbow.
BORACHIO	Mass, and my elbow itched: I thought there would a scab follow.

65

70

75

80

85

90

Borachio promises to share some secret information with Conrade.

93 **Stand thee close**: Stay hidden
pent-house: roof overhang
94 **true drunkard**: the name 'Borachio' means 'drunkard' in Spanish

99 **dear**: 1 expensive; 2 fine

102 **will**: want / demand

104 **unconfirmed**: inexperienced
104–6 **the fashion ... man**: i.e. clothes don't make the man

111 **deformed ... is**: i.e. people spend a fortune trying to keep up with changing fashions
112 **Deformed**: he misunderstands, thinking it is a man's name

Think about

- 'Borachio' means 'drunkard' in Spanish. What is there in this conversation that suggests that he might be drunk?

116 **vane**: weather-vane

120 **reechy**: dirty
121 **Bel**: Baal (an ancient god)

CONRADE	I will owe thee an answer for that. And now forward with thy tale.
BORACHIO	Stand thee close then under this pent-house, for it drizzles rain; and I will, like a true drunkard, utter all to thee. 95
WATCHMAN 2	(*Aside*) Some treason, masters: yet stand close.
BORACHIO	... Therefore know I have earned of Don John a thousand ducats.
CONRADE	Is it possible that any villainy should be so dear?
BORACHIO	Thou should'st rather ask if it were possible any villainy 100 should be so rich – for when rich villains have need of poor ones, poor ones may make what price they will.
CONRADE	I wonder at it.
BORACHIO	That shows thou art unconfirmed. Thou knowest that the fashion of a doublet, or a hat, or a cloak, is nothing to a 105 man.
CONRADE	Yes, it is apparel.
BORACHIO	I mean, the fashion.
CONRADE	Yes, the fashion is the fashion.
BORACHIO	Tush! I may as well say the fool's the fool. But see'st thou 110 not what a deformed thief this fashion is?
WATCHMAN 1	(*Aside*) I know that Deformed. 'A has been a vile thief this seven year. 'A goes up and down like a gentleman. I remember his name.
BORACHIO	Didst thou not hear somebody? 115
CONRADE	No; 'twas the vane on the house.
BORACHIO	See'st thou not, I say, what a deformed thief this fashion is, how giddily 'a turns about all the hot bloods between fourteen and five-and-thirty – some times fashioning them like Pharaoh's soldiers in the reechy painting, 120 sometime like god Bel's priests in the old church-

Borachio explains how he has tricked Claudio and Don Pedro into believing that Hero is unfaithful. The watchmen jump out and arrest Borachio and Conrade.

123 **smirched**: dirty
cod-piece: a fabric pouch attached to the front of the breeches
124 **massy**: enormous

135 **possessed**: given information
136 **amiable**: loving

140 **oaths**: sworn promises

146 **o'ernight**: last night

151 **recovered**: he means 'discovered'
lechery: sexual wickedness (he means 'treachery')
154 **lock**: long lock of hair

Think about

• The watchman claims to have 'recovered the most dangerous piece of lechery' (line 151). He presumably means that he has uncovered treachery – but in what way is his malapropism (use of the wrong word) oddly appropriate?

---

window, sometime like the shaven Hercules in the smirched worm-eaten tapestry, where his cod-piece seems as massy as his club?

CONRADE   All this I see. And I see that the fashion wears out more 125
apparel than the man. But art not thou thyself giddy with the fashion too, that thou hast shifted out of thy tale into telling me of the fashion?

BORACHIO   Not so, neither. But know that I have tonight wooed
Margaret, the Lady Hero's gentlewoman, by the name of 130
Hero. She leans me out at her mistress' chamber-
window, bids me a thousand times goodnight – I tell this tale vilely – I should first tell thee how the Prince, Claudio, and my master, planted, and placed, and possessed, by my master Don John, saw afar off in the 135
orchard this amiable encounter.

CONRADE   And thought they Margaret was Hero?

BORACHIO   Two of them did, the Prince and Claudio – but the devil
my master knew she was Margaret. And partly by his oaths, which first possessed them, partly by the dark 140
night, which did deceive them, but chiefly by my villainy, which did confirm any slander that Don John had made, away went Claudio enraged: swore he would meet her, as he was appointed, next morning at the temple, and there, before the whole congregation, 145
shame her with what he saw o'ernight, and send her home again without a husband.

WATCHMAN 1 (*Coming forward*) We charge you, in the Prince's name,
stand!

WATCHMAN 2 Call up the right Master Constable. We have here 150
recovered the most dangerous piece of lechery that ever was known in the commonwealth.

WATCHMAN 1 And one Deformed is one of them: I know him, 'a wears
a lock.

Borachio and Conrade are led
off to prison by the Watch.

158   **obey**: he means 'order'

160   **goodly commodity**: fine goods
160–1   **taken … bills**: 1 arrested by these
men's weapons; 2 bought on credit in
exchange for bonds
162   **in question**: 1 dubious; 2 much sought
after

Think about

• Borachio and Conrade
exchange word-play at the
end of this scene, in lines
160 to 163. What is its
effect as they are led away?

CONRADE	Masters, masters –	**155**
WATCHMAN 2	You'll be made bring Deformed forth, I warrant you.	
CONRADE	Masters –	
WATCHMAN 1	Never speak, we charge you. Let us obey you to go with us.	
BORACHIO	We are like to prove a goodly commodity, being taken up of these men's bills.	**160**
CONRADE	A commodity in question, I warrant you. (*To the* **WATCHMEN**) Come, we'll obey you.	

Exeunt.

RSC, 1982

National Theatre, 1981

RSC, 1976

RSC, 1988

In this scene ...

- Margaret helps Hero to prepare for the wedding.
- Beatrice arrives behaving miserably and claiming to have a cold.
- Margaret and Hero mock Beatrice for being love-sick.

Margaret is helping Hero to prepare for the wedding.

6 **Troth**: In truth
   rebato: a wired collar supporting a lace ruff

12 **tire**: head-dress

Think about

- What do characters say in this scene and in Act 3 Scene 2 about dress and fashion?

- Dress is part of outward appearance. Where in the play so far have people made mistakes by judging purely by outward appearance?

- Why does Hero say her heart is 'exceeding heavy' (lines 22 to 23)?

---

16 **exceeds**: is better than all others
17 **in respect of**: compared with
18 **cuts**: ornamental slashes in the fabric
    laced with silver: decorated with silver lace
19 **down-sleeves**: tight long sleeves
    side-sleeves: ornamental long sleeves hanging from the shoulders
19–20 **round ... tinsel**: lined with silvery-blue fabric
20 **quaint**: elegant
21 **on't**: of it
25 **Fie upon thee**: Shame on you

Inside Leonato's house.

Enter HERO, MARGARET, *and* URSULA.

HERO	Good Ursula, wake my cousin Beatrice, and desire her to rise.
URSULA	I will, lady.
HERO	And bid her come hither.
URSULA	Well.

5

Exit.

MARGARET	Troth, I think your other rebato were better.
HERO	No, pray thee, good Meg, I'll wear this.
MARGARET	By my troth, 's not so good, and I warrant your cousin will say so.
HERO	My cousin's a fool and thou art another. I'll wear none but this.

10

MARGARET	I like the new tire within excellently, if the hair were a thought browner. And your gown's a most rare fashion, i'faith. I saw the Duchess of Milan's gown that they praise so.

15

HERO	O, that exceeds, they say.
MARGARET	By my troth, 's but a nightgown in respect of yours – cloth o' gold, and cuts, and laced with silver, set with pearls, down-sleeves, side-sleeves, and skirts round underborne with a bluish tinsel. But for a fine, quaint, graceful and excellent fashion, yours is worth ten on't.

20

HERO	God give me joy to wear it, for my heart is exceeding heavy.
MARGARET	'Twill be heavier soon, by the weight of a man.
HERO	Fie upon thee! Art not ashamed?

25

Beatrice claims to be miserable
because she has a head-cold.

29   **saving your reverence**: begging your
     pardon
     An: If
     bad: bawdy / dirty
30   **wrest true speaking**: distort the
     meaning of honest words
33   **light**: immoral

35   **coz**: cousin

39   **Clap's into**: Let's sing
     Light o'Love: a popular dance tune
     burden: 1 bass harmony; 2 weight of a
     man
41   **light o'love**: a loose woman
     with your heels: 'light heels' was slang
     for an unchaste woman
42   **barnes**: barns (with word-play on
     'bairns' – children)
45–6 **Heigh-ho! ... husband?**: 'Heigh-ho'
     could be a hunting-call as well as a
     sighing sound.
47   **H**: the letter 'H' sounded like the word
     'ache'
48   **an ... Turk**: if you haven't changed
     your beliefs
48–9 **there's ... star**: i.e. you can't be certain
     of anything any more
50   **trow**: do you think

Think about

• The word 'stuffed', used in
  lines 54 and 55, clearly has
  a sexual meaning and
  Margaret's reply is intended
  as a joke. But what do we
  know about the plot which
  gives the joke a serious
  edge?

54   **am stuffed**: have a head-cold

55   **and stuffed**: i.e. having had sex, or
     pregnant

MARGARET	Of what, lady? Of speaking honourably? Is not marriage honourable in a beggar? Is not your lord honourable without marriage? I think you would have me say, 'saving your reverence, a husband'. An bad thinking do not wrest true speaking, I'll offend nobody. Is there any harm in 'the heavier for a husband'? None, I think, an it be the right husband and the right wife. Otherwise 'tis light, and not heavy. Ask my Lady Beatrice else: here she comes.

Enter BEATRICE.

HERO	Good morrow, coz.	35
BEATRICE	Good morrow, sweet Hero.	
HERO	Why, how now? Do you speak in the sick tune?	
BEATRICE	I am out of all other tune, methinks.	
MARGARET	Clap's into 'Light o'Love': that goes without a burden. Do you sing it, and I'll dance it.	40
BEATRICE	Ye light o'love with your heels! Then if your husband have stables enough, you'll see he shall lack no barnes.	
MARGARET	O illegitimate construction! I scorn that with my heels.	
BEATRICE	'Tis almost five o'clock, cousin: 'tis time you were ready. By my troth, I am exceeding ill. Heigh-ho!	45
MARGARET	For a hawk, a horse, or a husband?	
BEATRICE	For the letter that begins them all, H.	
MARGARET	Well, an you be not turned Turk, there's no more sailing by the star.	
BEATRICE	What means the fool, trow?	50
MARGARET	Nothing I: but God send everyone their heart's desire!	
HERO	These gloves the Count sent me: they are an excellent perfume.	
BEATRICE	I am stuffed, cousin; I cannot smell.	
MARGARET	A maid, and stuffed! There's goodly catching of cold.	55

Margaret teases Beatrice for being love-sick. The women rush off to finish dressing for the wedding.

57   **apprehension**: wit

59   **rarely**: excellently

62   **Carduus Benedictus**: a medicinal herb
63   **qualm**: sickness

65   **moral**: hidden meaning

70   **list**: please

76   **eats … grudging**: has an appetite and doesn't complain

80   **Not a false gallop**: i.e. I am speaking the truth.

Think about

- How does Margaret get the better of Beatrice's wit in this scene?

- How would you describe the different moods of Margaret, Hero and Beatrice here?

BEATRICE	O, God help me! God help me! How long have you professed apprehension?
MARGARET	Ever since you left it. Doth not my wit become me rarely?
BEATRICE	It is not seen enough. You should wear it in your cap. By my troth, I am sick.
MARGARET	Get you some of this distilled Carduus Benedictus, and lay it to your heart. It is the only thing for a qualm.
HERO	There thou prick'st her with a thistle.
BEATRICE	Benedictus! Why Benedictus? You have some moral in this 'Benedictus'?
MARGARET	Moral? No, by my troth, I have no moral meaning: I meant plain holy-thistle. You may think perchance that I think you are in love. Nay, by'r Lady, I am not such a fool to think what I list, nor I list not to think what I can – nor indeed I cannot think, if I would think my heart out of thinking, that you are in love, or that you will be in love, or that you can be in love. Yet Benedick was such another, and now is he become a man. He swore he would never marry, and yet now, in despite of his heart, he eats his meat without grudging. And how you may be converted I know not; but methinks you look with your eyes as other women do.
BEATRICE	What pace is this that thy tongue keeps?
MARGARET	Not a false gallop.

Enter URSULA.

URSULA	Madam, withdraw. The Prince, the Count, Signior Benedick, Don John and all the gallants of the town are come, to fetch you to church.
HERO	Help to dress me, good coz, good Meg, good Ursula.

Exeunt.

60

65

70

75

80

In this scene ...

- Dogberry and Verges visit Leonato to tell him about the arrest of Borachio and Conrade.
- Leonato receives their confused report, but is in too much of a hurry to investigate further.

Dogberry and Verges report to Leonato with important news. Dogberry's difficulty with words and self-importance prevent him from delivering his message.

2–3 **confidence ... decerns**: he means 'conference' ... 'concerns'

3 **nearly**: closely

8 **Goodman**: a title used of middle-class men

9 **blunt**: he means 'sharp'

14 **odorous**: he means 'odious' (hateful)
  palabras: few words (from Spanish)

Think about

- Dogberry clearly misunderstands Leonato's complaint that he is 'tedious' (line 15) and takes it as a compliment. Looking at his response (in lines 16 to 24) what does he appear to think it means?

22 **exclamation**: he means 'acclamation' (praise)

26 **fain**: like to

At Leonato's house.

Enter LEONATO, *with Constable* DOGBERRY, *and* VERGES.

LEONATO	What would you with me, honest neighbour?
DOGBERRY	Marry, sir, I would have some confidence with you that decerns you nearly.
LEONATO	Brief, I pray you – for you see it is a busy time with me.
DOGBERRY	Marry, this it is, sir.
VERGES	Yes, in truth it is, sir.
LEONATO	What is it, my good friends?
DOGBERRY	Goodman Verges, sir, speaks a little off the matter – an old man, sir, and his wits are not so blunt as, God help, I would desire they were – but, in faith, honest as the skin between his brows.
VERGES	Yes, I thank God I am as honest as any man living that is an old man and no honester than I.
DOGBERRY	Comparisons are odorous – palabras, neighbour Verges.
LEONATO	Neighbours, you are tedious.
DOGBERRY	It pleases your worship to say so, but we are the poor Duke's officers. But truly, for mine own part, if I were as tedious as a king, I could find it in my heart to bestow it all of your worship.
LEONATO	All thy tediousness on me, ah?
DOGBERRY	Yea, an 'twere a thousand pound more than 'tis, for I hear as good exclamation on your worship as of any man in the city. And though I be but a poor man, I am glad to hear it.
VERGES	And so am I.
LEONATO	I would fain know what you have to say.

5

10

15

20

25

Leonato has no time to spare. He asks Dogberry to question the prisoners himself.

28 **ta'en**: arrested
arrant knaves: complete villains

37 **he … you**: he's not in your class

41 **comprehended … aspicious**: he means 'apprehended' … 'suspicious'

Think about

• In lines 27 to 29, Verges comes close to giving Leonato the news that would avert disaster. How does this build the dramatic tension?

• What kind of character is Dogberry? Think about what causes him to interrupt Verges in lines 30 to 36.

• Dogberry, Verges and the Watch did not appear until Act 3 Scene 3. What purposes have they served in the play so far?

45 **suffigance**: he means 'sufficient'

47 **stay**: are waiting

49 **wait upon**: come to

55–6 **to a non-come**: out of their wits / bewildered
57 **excommunication**: he means 'examination'

VERGES	Marry, sir, our watch tonight, excepting your worship's presence, ha' ta'en a couple of as arrant knaves as any in Messina.
DOGBERRY	A good old man, sir, he will be talking. As they say, 'When the age is in, the wit is out'. God help us, it is a world to see! Well said, i'faith, neighbour Verges; well, God's a good man. An two men ride of a horse, one must ride behind. An honest soul, i' faith, sir, by my troth he is, as ever broke bread. But God is to be worshipped. All men are not alike. Alas, good neighbour!
LEONATO	Indeed, neighbour, he comes too short of you.
DOGBERRY	Gifts that God gives.
LEONATO	I must leave you.
DOGBERRY	One word, sir. Our watch, sir, have indeed comprehended two aspicious persons, and we would have them this morning examined before your worship.
LEONATO	Take their examination yourself and bring it me. I am now in great haste, as it may appear unto you.
DOGBERRY	It shall be suffigance.
LEONATO	Drink some wine ere you go. Fare you well!

Enter a MESSENGER.

MESSENGER	My lord, they stay for you to give your daughter to her husband.
LEONATO	I'll wait upon them: I am ready.

Exit LEONATO, *with* MESSENGER.

DOGBERRY	Go good partner, go, get you to Francis Seacoal. Bid him bring his pen and inkhorn to the jail. We are now to examination these men.
VERGES	And we must do it wisely.
DOGBERRY	We will spare for no wit, I warrant you. (*Pointing to his head*) Here's that shall drive some of them to a non-come. Only get the learnèd writer to set down our excommunication, and meet me at the jail.

Exeunt.

In this scene ...

- At the wedding Claudio claims that Hero is not a virgin.
- Hero faints. Leonato is furious at his daughter.
- The Friar does not believe that Hero is guilty. He suggests that they pretend she has died to make Claudio feel sorry.
- Beatrice and Benedick reveal their true feelings for one another.
- Benedick agrees to challenge Claudio to a duel.

Everyone assembles at the church to witness the wedding of Claudio and Hero. The service begins.

1 **plain form**: essentials

10 **conjoined**: united

Think about

- Leonato asks for only 'the plain form' of the marriage service (line 1). Why does he make this request, do you think?

- Why might it be better for the staging of the play only to have 'the plain form' in this scene, rather than the complete marriage service?

18–19 **Interjections ... he!**: Benedick's joke refers to grammar textbooks, where interjections or interruptions were listed according to the emotions expressed, e.g. laughing.

20 **thee by**: aside
by your leave: I beg your pardon

21 **unconstrainèd**: free / unforced

25 **counterpoise**: balance

In the church.

Enter DON PEDRO, DON JOHN, LEONATO, FRIAR FRANCIS, CLAUDIO, BENEDICK, HERO, BEATRICE *and* ATTENDANTS.

LEONATO	Come, Friar Francis, be brief: only to the plain form of marriage, and you shall recount their particular duties afterwards.
FRIAR	You come hither, my lord, to marry this lady?
CLAUDIO	No.
LEONATO	To be married *to* her, Friar! You come to marry her.
FRIAR	Lady, you come hither to be married to this Count?
HERO	I do.
FRIAR	If either of you know any inward impediment why you should not be conjoined, I charge you on your souls to utter it.
CLAUDIO	Know you any, Hero?
HERO	None, my lord.
FRIAR	Know you any, Count?
LEONATO	I dare make his answer: none.
CLAUDIO	O what men dare do! What men may do! What men daily do, not knowing what they do!
BENEDICK	How now! Interjections? Why, then, some be of laughing, as *ah, ha, he!*
CLAUDIO	Stand thee by, Friar. Father, by your leave: Will you with free and unconstrainèd soul Give me this maid, your daughter?
LEONATO	As freely, son, as God did give her me.
CLAUDIO	And what have I to give you back, whose worth May counterpoise this rich and precious gift?

Line numbers: 5, 10, 15, 20, 25

Claudio harshly announces that he will not marry Hero because she is not a virgin. Hero is bewildered and Leonato demands an explanation.

26 **render**: return

27 **learn**: teach

31 **maid**: virgin

35 **To witness**: as proof of

38 **luxurious**: lustful

41 **approvèd wanton**: proven whore

42 **proof**: test or trial of Hero

45 **known**: had sex with

47 **extenuate**: excuse

49 **large**: suggestive

51 **comely**: appropriate

53 **Out … Seeming**: Curse you for seeming innocent
    write … it: speak out against this kind of pretence

54 **Dian**: Diana, goddess of the moon and chastity

55 **be blown**: comes into bloom

57 **Venus**: goddess of love and sex

59 **wide**: wildly / wide of the mark

Think about

- In lines 32 to 33, Claudio describes Don John without realising it. Which other lines in this scene refer to appearance giving a misleading version of reality?

DON PEDRO	Nothing, unless you render her again.
CLAUDIO	Sweet Prince, you learn me noble thankfulness.
	There, Leonato, take her back again:
	Give not this rotten orange to your friend.
	She's but the sign and semblance of her honour.
	Behold how like a maid she blushes here!
	O, what authority and show of truth
	Can cunning sin cover itself withal!
	Comes not that blood as modest evidence
	To witness simple virtue? Would you not swear,
	All you that see her, that she were a maid
	By these exterior shows? But she is none.
	She knows the heat of a luxurious bed.
	Her blush is guiltiness, not modesty.
LEONATO	What do you mean, my lord?
CLAUDIO	Not to be married;
	Not to knit my soul to an approvèd wanton.
LEONATO	Dear my lord, if you in your own proof
	Have vanquished the resistance of her youth,
	And made defeat of her virginity –
CLAUDIO	I know what you would say. If I have known her,
	You will say she did embrace me as a husband,
	And so extenuate the 'forehand sin.
	No, Leonato,
	I never tempted her with word too large,
	But, as a brother to his sister, showed
	Bashful sincerity and comely love.
HERO	And seemed I ever otherwise to you?
CLAUDIO	Out on thee! Seeming! I will write against it.
	You seem to me as Dian in her orb,
	As chaste as is the bud ere it be blown.
	But you are more intemperate in your blood
	Than Venus, or those pampered animals
	That rage in savage sensuality.
HERO	Is my lord well, that he doth speak so wide?
LEONATO	Sweet Prince, why speak not you?

30

35

40

45

50

55

137

Don Pedro supports Claudio's slander, saying that they saw Hero speak to a man at her window the previous night.

61 gone about: worked hard
62 stale: prostitute

64 nuptial: wedding

71 kindly: natural

75 catechizing: questioning

---Think about---

• Hero is accused of 'talking' with a man 'at her chamber-window' (line 88). Have you formed an impression of Hero as a 'talkative' or a 'silent' character, compared with the other women? Look back at Act 2 Scene 1, lines 43 to 48 and lines 57 to 69, for example.

79 Hero … virtue: Hero has blotted her own name, which, in myth, stands for loyal love.

89 liberal: 1 coarse / foul-mouthed; 2 talkative

| DON PEDRO | What should I speak? | 60 |

I stand dishonoured, that have gone about
To link my dear friend to a common stale.

| LEONATO | Are these things spoken, or do I but dream? |

| DON JOHN | Sir, they are spoken; and these things are true. |

| BENEDICK | (*Aside*) This looks not like a nuptial. |

| HERO | True? O God! | 65 |

| CLAUDIO | Leonato, stand I here? |

Is this the Prince? Is this the Prince's brother?
Is this face Hero's? Are our eyes our own?

| LEONATO | All this is so: but what of this, my lord? |

| CLAUDIO | Let me but move one question to your daughter; | 70 |

And, by that fatherly and kindly power
That you have in her, bid her answer truly.

| LEONATO | I charge thee do so, as thou art my child. |

| HERO | O God defend me! How am I beset! |

What kind of catechizing call you this?   75

| CLAUDIO | To make you answer truly to your name. |

| HERO | Is it not Hero? Who can blot that name |

With any just reproach?

| CLAUDIO | Marry, that can Hero. |

Hero itself can blot out Hero's virtue.
What man was he talked with you yesternight   80
Out at your window betwixt twelve and one?
Now, if you are a maid, answer to this.

| HERO | I talked with no man at that hour, my lord. |

| DON PEDRO | Why, then are you no maiden. Leonato: |

I am sorry you must hear. Upon mine honour,   85
Myself, my brother, and this grievèd Count
Did see her, hear her, at that hour last night,
Talk with a ruffian at her chamber-window –
Who hath, indeed, most like a liberal villain,
Confessed the vile encounters they have had   90
A thousand times in secret.

Hero faints. Don Pedro, Don John and Claudio leave but Benedick stays to help her.

95 **misgovernment**: bad behaviour

100 **impious**: unholy
101 **For thee**: Because of you
gates of love: heart, eyes, mind (i.e. the ways in which love might come to him)
102 **conjecture**: suspicion

106 **Wherefore**: Why

108 **Smother ... up**: i.e. cause her to faint

Think about

- What words or actions appear to be the last straw for Hero, causing her to faint (lines 105 to 106)?

- Look at lines 108 to 109. Why do you think Benedick stays behind rather than leaving with the other men? List the conflicting reasons he might have for (a) leaving with Don Pedro and (b) staying behind.

---

114 **look up**: 1 open your eyes, i.e. recover; 2 i.e. to heaven, as though she were innocent

DON JOHN	Fie, fie, they are
	Not to be named, my lord, not to be spoke of!
	There is not chastity enough in language
	Without offence to utter them. Thus, pretty lady,
	I am sorry for thy much misgovernment. **95**
CLAUDIO	O Hero! What a Hero hadst thou been,
	If half thy outward graces had been placed
	About thy thoughts and counsels of thy heart!
	But fare thee well, most foul, most fair! Farewell,
	Thou pure impiety and impious purity! **100**
	For thee I'll lock up all the gates of love,
	And on my eyelids shall conjecture hang,
	To turn all beauty into thoughts of harm,
	And never shall it more be gracious.
LEONATO	Hath no man's dagger here a point for me? **105**

HERO faints.

BEATRICE	Why, how now, cousin! Wherefore sink you down?
DON JOHN	Come, let us go. These things, come thus to light,
	Smother her spirits up.

Exit DON PEDRO, with DON JOHN and CLAUDIO.

BENEDICK	How doth the lady?
BEATRICE	Dead, I think. Help, uncle!
	Hero! Why, Hero! Uncle! Signior Benedick! Friar! **110**
LEONATO	O Fate! Take not away thy heavy hand.
	Death is the fairest cover for her shame
	That may be wished for.

HERO stirs.

BEATRICE	How now, cousin Hero?
FRIAR	Have comfort, lady.
LEONATO	Dost thou look up?
FRIAR	Yea, wherefore should she not? **115**

Leonato is furious and ashamed at the accusation. He believes it because it came from Don Pedro and Claudio.

118   **printed ... blood**: 1 revealed by her blushes; 2 part of her nature

122   **on the rearward of**: immediately following

124   **Chid ... frame**: Did I reproach nature for giving me only one child

128   **issue**: child

129   **smirchèd ... mired ...**: dirtied ... muddied ...

132–4   **But mine ... not mine**: Leonato's grief and shame are mainly based on how extremely he has loved Hero and on how her disgrace reflects on him.

138   **salt**: salt was used to preserve meat to stop it rotting

140   **attired**: wrapped

142   **belied**: slandered

143   **bedfellow**: someone who shared a bed

Think about

- In your opinion, what is the worst thing Leonato says in his outburst at his daughter (lines 116 to 150)?

- In what ways might audiences' impressions of Leonato change during this scene, compared with their view of him before this scene?

LEONATO	Wherefore! Why, doth not every earthly thing
	Cry shame upon her? Could she here deny
	The story that is printed in her blood?
	Do not live, Hero, do not ope thine eyes:
	For, did I think thou would'st not quickly die, 120
	Thought I thy spirits were stronger than thy shames,
	Myself would, on the rearward of reproaches,
	Strike at thy life. Grieved I, I had but one?
	Chid I for that at frugal Nature's frame?
	O, one too much by thee! Why had I one? 125
	Why ever wast thou lovely in my eyes?
	Why had I not with charitable hand
	Took up a beggar's issue at my gates,
	Who, smirchèd thus and mired with infamy,
	I might have said 'No part of it is mine: 130
	This shame derives itself from unknown loins'?
	But mine, and mine I loved and mine I praised,
	And mine that I was proud on – mine so much
	That I myself was to myself not mine,
	Valuing of her – why, she, O, she is fallen 135
	Into a pit of ink, that the wide sea
	Hath drops too few to wash her clean again,
	And salt too little which may season give
	To her foul tainted flesh!
BENEDICK	Sir, sir, be patient.
	For my part, I am so attired in wonder, 140
	I know not what to say.
BEATRICE	O, on my soul, my cousin is belied!
BENEDICK	Lady, were you her bedfellow last night?
BEATRICE	No, truly not – although, until last night,
	I have this twelvemonth been her bedfellow. 145
LEONATO	Confirmed, confirmed! O, that is stronger made
	Which was before barred up with ribs of iron!
	Would the two Princes lie, and Claudio lie,
	Who loved her so, that, speaking of her foulness,
	Washed it with tears? Hence from her: let her die! 150

The Friar stands up for Hero and tries to get at the truth. Benedick begins to suspect Don John of some sort of villainous trick.

155 **apparitions**: appearances

162–3 **Which ... book**: i.e. my experience and learning back up my observation
164 **divinity**: status as a holy man

169 **perjury**: lying under oath

171 **That ... nakedness**: i.e. Hero's unfaithfulness, which has been clearly exposed

175 **warrant**: allow

178 **unmeet**: improper / inappropriate
179 **Maintained ... words**: talked

181 **misprision**: misunderstanding

182 **have ... honour**: are absolutely honourable

184 **practice**: plotting
185 **in frame of**: devising

---Think about---
- Often when people have powerful emotions to express in Shakespeare's plays, they use simple words. Look at lines 166 to 168 ('Friar, it ... damnation'). How does the fact that the last word is the only long one make it sound even worse?

FRIAR	Hear me a little.
	For I have only silent been so long,
	And given way unto this course of fortune
	By noting of the lady. I have marked
	A thousand blushing apparitions 155
	To start into her face, a thousand innocent shames
	In angel whiteness beat away those blushes.
	And in her eye there hath appeared a fire,
	To burn the errors that these Princes hold
	Against her maiden truth. Call me a fool; 160
	Trust not my reading nor my observations,
	Which with experimental seal doth warrant
	The tenor of my book; trust not my age,
	My reverence, calling, nor divinity,
	If this sweet lady lie not guiltless here 165
	Under some biting error.
LEONATO	Friar, it cannot be.
	Thou see'st that all the grace that she hath left
	Is that she will not add to her damnation
	A sin of perjury: she not denies it.
	Why seek'st thou then to cover with excuse 170
	That which appears in proper nakedness?
FRIAR	Lady, what man is he you are accused of?
HERO	They know that do accuse me. I know none.
	If I know more of any man alive
	Than that which maiden modesty doth warrant, 175
	Let all my sins lack mercy! O my father,
	Prove you that any man with me conversed
	At hours unmeet, or that I yesternight
	Maintained the change of words with any creature,
	Refuse me, hate me, torture me to death! 180
FRIAR	There is some strange misprision in the Princes.
BENEDICK	Two of them have the very bent of honour;
	And if their wisdoms be misled in this,
	The practice of it lives in John the bastard,
	Whose spirits toil in frame of villainies. 185

The Friar advises them to pretend that Hero has died. The aim is to win sympathy for Hero, and to make Claudio feel sorry.

190 **eat**: eaten
invention: intelligence
192 **reft**: deprived
193 **in such a kind**: to such a degree

196 **quit ... throughly**: pay them back completely

201 **mourning ostentation**: formal show of grief

209 **on ... birth**: look for something better to come out of this

---
Think about

- If you were the director, how would you ask Leonato and Hero to act towards one another throughout the scene? Think about the way Leonato has treated Hero in earlier scenes.

213 **falls out**: happens
214 **prize ... worth**: do not appreciate its real value
216 **rack**: exaggerate

221 **study of imagination**: brooding thoughts
222 **organ**: aspect
223 **habit**: clothing

LEONATO	I know not. If they speak but truth of her,
	These hands shall tear her. If they wrong her honour,
	The proudest of them shall well hear of it.
	Time hath not yet so dried this blood of mine,
	Nor age so eat up my invention,

190

Nor fortune made such havoc of my means,
Nor my bad life reft me so much of friends,
But they shall find, awaked in such a kind,
Both strength of limb and policy of mind,
Ability in means and choice of friends   195
To quit me of them throughly.

FRIAR   Pause awhile,
And let my counsel sway you in this case.
Your daughter here the Princes left for dead.
Let her awhile be secretly kept in,
And publish it that she is dead indeed.   200
Maintain a mourning ostentation;
And on your family's old monument
Hang mournful epitaphs, and do all rites
That appertain unto a burial.

LEONATO   What shall become of this? What will this do?   205

FRIAR   Marry, this, well carried, shall on her behalf
Change slander to remorse: that is some good.
But not for that dream I on this strange course,
But on this travail look for greater birth.
She dying, as it must be so maintained,   210
Upon the instant that she was accused,
Shall be lamented, pitied, and excused
Of every hearer: for it so falls out
That what we have we prize not to the worth
Whiles we enjoy it; but being lacked and lost,   215
Why, then we rack the value, then we find
The virtue that possession would not show us
Whiles it was ours. So will it fare with Claudio.
When he shall hear she died upon his words,
Th' idea of her life shall sweetly creep   220
Into his study of imagination.
And every lovely organ of her life
Shall come apparelled in more precious habit,

Everyone agrees to the Friar's plan. Beatrice and Benedick are left alone for the first time since they discovered their love for one another.

227 **interest in**: claim to
liver: supposedly the origin of love

230 **doubt**: fear

233 **all ... false**: all the rest of my plan fails

236 **sort**: turns out

238 **some ... life**: i.e. in a nunnery

241 **inwardness**: close friendship

245 **Being ... grief**: Since I am overwhelmed by grief

248 **to ... cure**: desperate diseases need desperate remedies
250 **prolonged**: postponed

Think about

- How does the Friar assume that Claudio will take the news of Hero's death?

- What do you think of the Friar's 'plan B' (see lines 236 to 239)?

	More moving, delicate, and full of life,	
	Into the eye and prospect of his soul,	225
	Than when she lived indeed. Then shall he mourn,	
	If ever love had interest in his liver,	
	And wish he had not so accusèd her –	
	No, though he thought his accusation true.	
	Let this be so, and doubt not but success	230
	Will fashion the event in better shape	
	Than I can lay it down in likelihood.	
	But if all aim but this be levelled false,	
	The supposition of the lady's death	
	Will quench the wonder of her infamy.	235
	And if it sort not well, you may conceal her,	
	As best befits her wounded reputation,	
	In some reclusive and religious life,	
	Out of all eyes, tongues, minds, and injuries.	
BENEDICK	Signior Leonato, let the Friar advise you.	240
	And though you know my inwardness and love	
	Is very much unto the Prince and Claudio,	
	Yet, by mine honour, I will deal in this	
	As secretly and justly as your soul	
	Should with your body.	
LEONATO	Being that I flow in grief,	245
	The smallest twine may lead me.	
FRIAR	'Tis well consented. Presently away:	
	For to strange sores strangely they strain the cure.	
	Come, lady, die to live. This wedding-day	
	Perhaps is but prolonged: have patience and endure.	250

All exit except BENEDICK *and* BEATRICE.

BENEDICK	Lady Beatrice, have you wept all this while?	
BEATRICE	Yea, and I will weep a while longer.	
BENEDICK	I will not desire that.	
BEATRICE	You have no reason: I do it freely.	
BENEDICK	Surely I do believe your fair cousin is wronged.	255
BEATRICE	Ah, how much might the man deserve of me that would right her!	

Beatrice and Benedick declare their love for each other. She asks him to kill Claudio for what he has done to Hero, but he refuses at first.

259 **even**: clear
no ... friend: I have no such friend

261 **office**: job

269 **and eat it**: and then have to eat your words (i.e. go back on your promise)

273 **protest**: declare

277 **stayed ... hour**: stopped me just in time

---Think about---

• Beatrice tells Benedick that getting revenge for Hero's shaming is 'a man's office, but not yours' (line 261). Why might she feel that Benedick is not the man to fight Claudio?

• 'Kill Claudio' often gets a laugh, though Beatrice is completely serious. In a recent production, Beatrice and Benedick looked at the audience, startled that they were laughing. Why might the audience laugh? Is this an appropriate response?

286 **Tarry**: Wait a moment

BENEDICK	Is there any way to show such friendship?	
BEATRICE	A very even way, but no such friend.	
BENEDICK	May a man do it?	260
BEATRICE	It is a man's office, but not yours.	
BENEDICK	I do love nothing in the world so well as you. Is not that strange?	
BEATRICE	As strange as the thing I know not. It were as possible for me to say I loved nothing so well as you. But believe me not, and yet I lie not: I confess nothing, nor I deny nothing. I am sorry for my cousin.	265
BENEDICK	By my sword, Beatrice, thou lovest me.	
BEATRICE	Do not swear and eat it.	
BENEDICK	I will swear by it that you love me; and I will make him eat it that says I love not you.	270
BEATRICE	Will you not eat your word?	
BENEDICK	With no sauce that can be devised to it. I protest I love thee.	
BEATRICE	Why, then, God forgive me!	275
BENEDICK	What offence, sweet Beatrice?	
BEATRICE	You have stayed me in a happy hour. I was about to protest I loved *you*.	
BENEDICK	And do it with all thy heart.	
BEATRICE	I love you with so much of my heart that none is left to protest.	280
BENEDICK	Come, bid me do anything for thee.	
BEATRICE	Kill Claudio.	
BENEDICK	Ha! Not for the wide world.	
BEATRICE	You kill me to deny it. Farewell.	285
BENEDICK	Tarry, sweet Beatrice.	

Beatrice is furious that Claudio could get away with slandering Hero. She wishes she were a man so that she could fight Claudio herself.

295 **approved ... height**: proved in the highest degree

297 **bear ... hand**: lead her on

298 **take hands**: be joined in marriage

299 **unmitigated rancour**: bitterest hatred

302 **A proper saying**: A likely story

Think about

- In lines 286 to 288 ('Tarry ... let me go'), Shakespeare gives the actors stage directions through the dialogue. What should they do here?

- At which point do you think Benedick starts to come round to the idea that he must challenge Claudio? What changes his mind?

307 **counties**: counts

308 **Comfect**: Candy

311 **curtsies**: formal, empty gestures

311–12 **only ... tongue**: all talk

312 **trim**: attractive but insincere

BEATRICE	I am gone though I am here. There is no love in you. Nay, I pray you, let me go.
BENEDICK	Beatrice –
BEATRICE	In faith, I will go. 290
BENEDICK	We'll be friends first.
BEATRICE	You dare easier be friends with me than fight with mine enemy.
BENEDICK	Is Claudio thine enemy?
BEATRICE	Is he not approved in the height a villain that hath 295 slandered, scorned, dishonoured my kinswoman? O that I were a man! What, bear her in hand until they come to take hands, and then, with public accusation, uncovered slander, unmitigated rancour – O God, that I were a man! I would eat his heart in the market-place. 300
BENEDICK	Hear me, Beatrice –
BEATRICE	Talk with a man out at a window! A proper saying!
BENEDICK	Nay, but Beatrice –
BEATRICE	Sweet Hero! She is wronged, she is slandered, she is undone. 305
BENEDICK	Beat –
BEATRICE	Princes and counties! Surely, a princely testimony, a goodly count, Count Comfect – a sweet gallant, surely! O that I were a man for his sake, or that I had any friend would be a man for my sake! But manhood is melted 310 into curtsies, valour into compliment; and men are only turned into tongue, and trim ones too. He is now as valiant as Hercules that only tells a lie and swears it. I cannot be a man with wishing: therefore I will die a woman with grieving. 315
BENEDICK	Tarry, good Beatrice. By this hand, I love thee.
BEATRICE	Use it for my love some other way than swearing by it.
BENEDICK	Think you in your soul the Count Claudio hath wronged Hero?

Benedick agrees to challenge
Claudio to a duel.

321   **engaged**: i.e. to fight Claudio

323   **dear**: costly, i.e. Claudio is going to
have to pay for this

Think about

• When Benedick says 'By this
hand...' (line 322), whose
hand is he swearing by?

• How is this oath different
from 'By my sword' (line
268)?

BEATRICE   Yea, as sure as I have a thought or a soul.   320

BENEDICK   Enough: I am engaged. I will challenge him. I will kiss
your hand, and so I leave you. By this hand, Claudio
shall render me a dear account. As you hear of me, so
think of me. Go, comfort your cousin: I must say she is
dead; and so, farewell.   325

Exeunt.

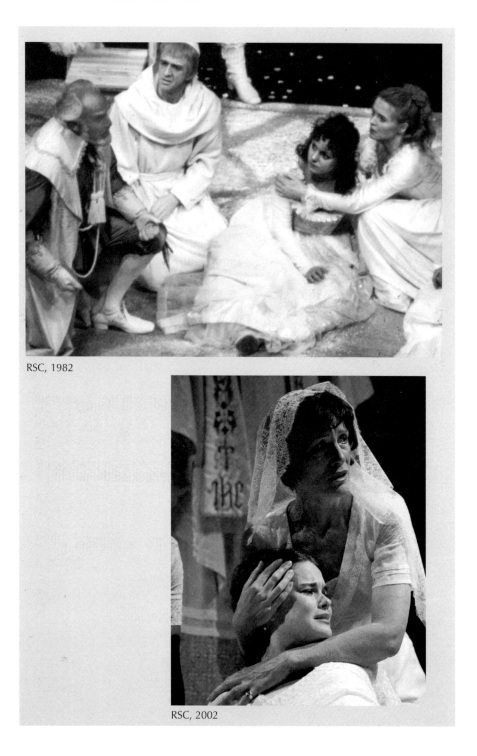

RSC, 1982

RSC, 2002

RSC, 1996

RSC, 1976

In this scene ...

- The Sexton questions Borachio and Conrade.
- The watchmen reveal what they know about Don John's plans to shame Hero.
- The Sexton announces that Don John has fled and that Hero has died.

Dogberry and Verges bring Borachio and Conrade before the Sexton for questioning.

s.d. gowns: i.e. magistrates' robes
  1 **dissembly**: he means 'assembly'
  2 **Sexton**: a church official
  3 **malefactors**: wrong-doers

  5 **exhibition**: he means 'commission' (official order)

 11 **sirrah**: a form of address to social inferiors

---**Think about**---

- Why does Conrade need to inform Dogberry 'I am a gentleman, sir' before he gives his name in line 12? Think about Dogberry's use of 'sirrah' in line 11.

 17 **defend**: forbid

- What do we expect to happen when we see Dogberry taking charge of the questioning of Borachio and Conrade?

 23 **go about with**: outsmart

A prison.

Enter DOGBERRY, VERGES *and the* SEXTON *in gowns; and men of the Watch, with* CONRADE *and* BORACHIO.

DOGBERRY	Is our whole dissembly appeared?
VERGES	O, a stool and a cushion for the Sexton.
SEXTON	Which be the malefactors?
DOGBERRY	Marry, that am I and my partner.
VERGES	Nay, that's certain. We have the exhibition to examine. 5
SEXTON	But which are the offenders that are to be examined? Let them come before Master Constable.
DOGBERRY	Yea, marry, let them come before me. What is your name, friend?
BORACHIO	Borachio. 10
DOGBERRY	Pray, write down 'Borachio'. Yours, sirrah?
CONRADE	I am a gentleman, sir, and my name is Conrade.
DOGBERRY	Write down 'Master Gentleman Conrade'. Masters, do you serve God?
CONRADE AND BORACHIO	Yea, sir, we hope. 15
DOGBERRY	Write down that they hope they serve God – and write 'God' first, for God defend but God should go before such villains! Masters, it is proved already that you are little better than false knaves, and it will go near to be thought so shortly. How answer you for yourselves? 20
CONRADE	Marry, sir, we say we are none.
DOGBERRY	*(To the* SEXTON *and* VERGES*)* A marvellous witty fellow, I assure you. But I will go about with him. *(To* BORACHIO*)* Come you hither, sirrah: a word in your ear. Sir, I say to you, it is thought you are false knaves. 25

The watchmen speak up and give the Sexton the important details of Borachio's villainy.

27 **in a tale**: telling the same story

31 **eftest**: quickest / easiest

36 **flat**: blatant / obvious
37 **perjury**: lying on oath (he probably means 'slander')

42 **Marry**: By the Virgin Mary

Think about

- What does Dogberry get wrong in this scene? Think about (a) his language (b) his incorrect legal procedures and (c) the crime he believes Borachio and Conrade to have committed.

51 **redemption**: being saved from sin (he means 'damnation')

BORACHIO   Sir, I say to you we are none.

DOGBERRY   Well, stand aside. 'Fore God, they are both in a tale. Have you writ down that they are none?

SEXTON   Master Constable, you go not the way to examine. You must call forth the watch that are their accusers.   30

DOGBERRY   Yea, marry, that's the eftest way: let the watch come forth. Masters, I charge you in the Prince's name, accuse these men.

WATCHMAN 1   This man said, sir, that Don John, the Prince's brother, was a villain.   35

DOGBERRY   Write down Prince John a villain. Why, this is flat perjury, to call a Prince's brother villain.

BORACHIO   Master Constable –

DOGBERRY   Pray thee, fellow, peace. I do not like thy look, I promise thee.   40

SEXTON   What heard you him say else?

WATCHMAN 2   Marry, that he had received a thousand ducats of Don John for accusing the Lady Hero wrongfully.

DOGBERRY   Flat burglary as ever was committed.

VERGES   Yea, by mass, that it is.   45

SEXTON   What else, fellow?

WATCHMAN 1   And that Count Claudio did mean, upon his words, to disgrace Hero before the whole assembly, and not marry her.

DOGBERRY   O villain! Thou wilt be condemned into everlasting   50
redemption for this.

SEXTON   What else?

WATCHMAN 2   This is all.

The Sexton tells Borachio that Hero has died because of his actions. As Conrade and Borachio are being led away, Conrade calls Dogberry an ass.

60 opinioned: he means 'pinioned' (bound)

62 coxcomb: fool

65 naughty varlet: wicked (much stronger than modern 'naughty') rogue

67 suspect: he means 'respect'

71 piety: he means 'impiety' (badness)

74–5 pretty … flesh: handsome a man

76 go to: I'll have you know

Think about

- How would you direct the actors playing Borachio and Conrade about how to react to the news of Hero's death? Should Borachio show some remorse, for example? (Bear in mind your decisions, and revise them if necessary, when you read Act 5 Scene 1, lines 217 to 249.)

- Dogberry's final speech (lines 67 to 79) is a great comic moment, but it also reveals details about his life. What does he say which makes us feel sympathy for him and helps us to see him as a rounded human being?

SEXTON	And this is more, masters, than you can deny. Prince John is this morning secretly stolen away. Hero was in 55 this manner accused, in this very manner refused, and upon the grief of this suddenly died. Master Constable, let these men be bound, and brought to Leonato's. I will go before and show him their examination.

Exit.

DOGBERRY	Come, let them be opinioned. 60
VERGES	Let them be in the hands –
CONRADE	Off, coxcomb!
DOGBERRY	God's my life, where's the Sexton? Let him write down the Prince's officer coxcomb. Come, bind them. Thou naughty varlet! 65
CONRADE	Away! You are an ass, you are an ass.
DOGBERRY	Dost thou not suspect my place? Dost thou not suspect my years? O that he were here to write me down an ass! But, masters, remember that I am an ass: though it be not written down, yet forget not that I am an ass. No, 70 thou villain, thou art full of piety, as shall be proved upon thee by good witness. I am a wise fellow, and, which is more, an officer; and, which is more, a householder; and, which is more, as pretty a piece of flesh as any is in Messina; and one that knows the law, 75 go to; and a rich fellow enough, go to; and a fellow that hath had losses; and one that hath two gowns and everything handsome about him. Bring him away. O that I had been writ down an ass!

Exeunt.

In this scene ...

- Leonato is extremely upset that Hero has been disgraced. He and Antonio both challenge Claudio to a duel.
- Benedick enters and also challenges Claudio to a duel.
- When Dogberry and Verges arrive with their prisoners, Borachio confesses.
- Claudio begs Leonato to forgive him and agrees to marry Antonio's daughter.

Leonato is devastated. His brother Antonio tries to console him.

2   **second**: assist

3   **counsel**: advice

7   **do suit with**: are the same as

12   **strain**: strong emotion

14   **lineament**: feature
16   **sorry wag**: poor fool
     cry 'hem!': clear the throat
17   **Patch**: Bandage
17–18 **make ... candle-wasters**: drown grief by studying philosophy

Think about

- Some would say that Leonato was unforgivably harsh to Hero in the church scene (Act 4 Scene 1). Do you think the sorrow he seems to be expressing here is for Hero or for himself? How do you know?

- What are your feelings about Leonato?

24   **preceptial medicine**: helpful advice
25   **Fetter**: Bind
26   **air**: i.e. empty words
27   **office**: duty
28   **wring**: writhe with pain
29   **sufficiency**: ability
30   **moral**: full of moral advice

32   **advertisement**: good advice

In front of Leonato's house.

Enter Leonato *and his brother* Antonio.

Antonio	If you go on thus, you will kill yourself;
	And 'tis not wisdom thus to second grief
	Against yourself.
Leonato	I pray thee, cease thy counsel,

Which falls into mine ears as profitless
As water in a sieve. Give not me counsel,   5
Nor let no comforter delight mine ear
But such a one whose wrongs do suit with mine.
Bring me a father that so loved his child,
Whose joy of her is overwhelmed like mine,
And bid him speak of patience.   10
Measure his woe the length and breadth of mine,
And let it answer every strain for strain,
As thus for thus, and such a grief for such,
In every lineament, branch, shape, and form.
If such a one will smile and stroke his beard,   15
And, sorry wag, cry 'hem!' when he should groan,
Patch grief with proverbs, make misfortune drunk
With candle-wasters – bring him yet to me,
And I of him will gather patience.
But there is no such man. For, brother, men   20
Can counsel and speak comfort to that grief
Which they themselves not feel – but, tasting it,
Their counsel turns to passion, which before
Would give preceptial medicine to rage,
Fetter strong madness in a silken thread,   25
Charm ache with air and agony with words.
No, no: 'tis all men's office to speak patience
To those that wring under the load of sorrow,
But no man's virtue nor sufficiency
To be so moral when he shall endure   30
The like himself. Therefore give me no counsel:
My griefs cry louder than advertisement.

Antonio	Therein do men from children nothing differ.

Leonato accuses Claudio of villainy.

37 writ the style of gods: written in a god-like manner
38 made ... at: scorned
chance and sufferance: fortune and enduring pain

42 belied: slandered

46 Good-e'en: Good afternoon (or evening)

Think about

- Who, earlier in the play, has expressed a view similar to Leonato's about toothache (lines 35 to 36)? Look at the opening of Act 3 Scene 2. Why is this an important idea in the play?

- In line 53, Leonato addresses Claudio as 'thou' instead of 'you' (the polite form he used in Act 1 Scene 1). In other contexts it can be a sign of friendship, but how is he using it here when he addresses Claudio?

---

49 all is one: it doesn't matter

53 dissembler: deceiver

55 beshrew: curse

57 meant ... to: did not mean anything in moving to

LEONATO	I pray thee, peace. I will be flesh and blood.
	For there was never yet philosopher 35
	That could endure the toothache patiently,
	However they have writ the style of gods,
	And made a push at chance and sufferance.
ANTONIO	Yet bend not all the harm upon yourself:
	Make those that do offend you suffer too. 40
LEONATO	There thou speak'st reason. Nay, I will do so.
	My soul doth tell me Hero is belied,
	And that shall Claudio know: so shall the Prince,
	And all of them that thus dishonour her.
ANTONIO	Here comes the Prince and Claudio hastily. 45

Enter DON PEDRO *and* CLAUDIO.

DON PEDRO	Good-e'en, good-e'en.
CLAUDIO	Good day to both of you.
LEONATO	Hear you, my lords!
DON PEDRO	We have some haste, Leonato.
LEONATO	Some haste, my lord! Well, fare you well, my lord.
	Are you so hasty now? Well, all is one.
DON PEDRO	Nay, do not quarrel with us, good old man. 50
ANTONIO	If he could right himself with quarrelling,
	Some of us would lie low.
CLAUDIO	Who wrongs him?
LEONATO	Marry, *thou* dost wrong me, thou dissembler, thou!
	– Nay, never lay thy hand upon thy sword:
	I fear thee not.
CLAUDIO	Marry, beshrew my hand 55
	If it should give your age such cause of fear.
	In faith, my hand meant nothing to my sword.

Leonato challenges Claudio to a duel.

58 **fleer**: scorn
59 **dotard**: foolish old man

64 **lay ... by**: put aside my dignity (as an older man)
66 **trial of a man**: i.e. a duel

71 **framed**: i.e. caused

75 **nice fence**: clever skills at fencing
76 **lustihood**: physical fitness

78 **daff me**: brush me aside

Think about

- Do Claudio's reactions here suggest that this is the first time he has heard of Hero's death, or do you think he has already been told?

- What quality of Claudio's character is Leonato insulting in the expression 'his nice fence' (line 75)?

82 **Win ... me**: Let him beat me first, then he can boast about it

84 **foining**: thrusting (a fencing term)

LEONATO	Tush, tush, man, never fleer and jest at me!
	I speak not like a dotard nor a fool,
	As under privilege of age to brag 60
	What I have done being young, or what would do
	Were I not old. Know, Claudio, to thy head,
	Thou hast so wronged mine innocent child and me
	That I am forced to lay my reverence by,
	And with grey hairs and bruise of many days 65
	Do challenge thee to trial of a man.
	I say thou hast belied mine innocent child.
	Thy slander hath gone through and through her heart,
	And she lies buried with her ancestors –
	O, in a tomb where never scandal slept, 70
	Save this of hers, framed by thy villainy!
CLAUDIO	My villainy?
LEONATO	Thine, Claudio; thine, I say.
DON PEDRO	You say not right, old man.
LEONATO	My lord, my lord,
	I'll prove it on his body if he dare,
	Despite his nice fence and his active practice, 75
	His May of youth and bloom of lustihood.
CLAUDIO	Away! I will not have to do with you.
LEONATO	Canst thou so daff me? Thou hast killed my child.
	If thou kill'st me, boy, thou shalt kill a man.
ANTONIO	He shall kill two of us, and men indeed; 80
	But that's no matter; let him kill one first.
	Win me and wear me: let him answer *me*.
	(*To* CLAUDIO) Come, follow me, boy: come, sir boy,
	come, follow me.
	Sir boy, I'll whip you from your foining fence –
	Nay, as I am a gentleman, I will. 85
LEONATO	Brother –

Antonio offers to fight Claudio as well.

89 answer a man: back up their words

91 apes: fashionable fools
jacks: scoundrels
milksops: wimps
94 scruple: smallest bit
95 Scambling: Unruly
out-facing: brazen
fashion-monging: shallow / faddish
96 cog: cheat
97 Go anticly: Follow bizarre fashions
show … hideousness: put on a threatening appearance

103 wake: try

Think about

• Don Pedro is the highest status character in the play. How should he say 'I will not hear you' (line 107)? How would you direct Leonato to react?

109 smart: hurt / suffer

• What direction would you give to the actors playing Claudio and Don Pedro about how they should react after the departure of Leonato and Antonio, and on Benedick's arrival at line 110?

ANTONIO	Content yourself. God knows I loved my niece;
	And she is dead, slandered to death by villains,
	That dare as well answer a man indeed
	As I dare take a serpent by the tongue. 90
	Boys, apes, braggarts, jacks, milksops!
LEONATO	Brother Antony –
ANTONIO	Hold you content. What, man! I know them, yea,
	And what they weigh, even to the utmost scruple –
	Scambling, out-facing, fashion-monging boys, 95
	That lie and cog and flout, deprave and slander,
	Go anticly, show outward hideousness,
	And speak off half a dozen dangerous words,
	How they might hurt their enemies, if they durst.
	And this is all. 100
LEONATO	But brother Antony –
ANTONIO	Come, 'tis no matter;
	Do not you meddle: let me deal in this.
DON PEDRO	Gentlemen both, we will not wake your patience.
	My heart is sorry for your daughter's death –
	But, on my honour, she was charged with nothing 105
	But what was true and very full of proof.
LEONATO	My lord, my lord –
DON PEDRO	I will not hear you.
LEONATO	No?
	Come brother, away. I will be heard.
ANTONIO	And shall, or some of us will smart for it.

Exit LEONATO, *with* ANTONIO.

DON PEDRO	See, see: here comes the man we went to seek. 110

Enter BENEDICK.

CLAUDIO	Now, signior, what news?
BENEDICK	Good day, my lord.

Don Pedro and Claudio try to joke with Benedick but he treats them coldly.

115   had like: were likely

122   high-proof: extremely
fain: like to

126–7   beside their wit: out of their minds
127   minstrels: musicians (who 'draw' bows across their strings)

Think about

- Benedick's expression 'in the career' (line 133) is a term from jousting (a sport played on horseback with lances), meaning 'at full speed'. How else does the language he uses in lines 119 to 124 hint that he is about to challenge Claudio?

- Don Pedro and Claudio mainly use the familiar 'thou' (rather than the polite 'you' form) to Benedick, as they are of similar status and have been friends (in lines 117, 121, 123, 125 and 130). How does Benedick reply?

131   care ... cat: i.e. worrying too much is bad for you (proverb)
132   mettle: spirit
133   in the career: at full speed

135   staff: lance
135–6   staff ... cross: i.e. his lance was snapped

139   how ... girdle: he'll have to put up with it / what he can do about it

DON PEDRO	Welcome, signior. You are almost come to part almost a fray.
CLAUDIO	We had like to have had our two noses snapped off with two old men without teeth. 115
DON PEDRO	Leonato and his brother. What think'st thou? Had we fought, I doubt we should have been too young for them.
BENEDICK	In a false quarrel there is no true valour. I came to seek you both. 120
CLAUDIO	We have been up and down to seek thee; for we are high-proof melancholy, and would fain have it beaten away. Wilt thou use thy wit?
BENEDICK	It is in my scabbard: shall I draw it?
DON PEDRO	Dost thou wear thy wit by thy side? 125
CLAUDIO	Never any did so, though very many have been beside their wit. I will bid thee draw, as we do the minstrels – draw to pleasure us.
DON PEDRO	As I am an honest man, he looks pale. (*To* BENEDICK) Art thou sick, or angry? 130
CLAUDIO	What, courage, man! What though care killed a cat, thou hast mettle enough in thee to kill care.
BENEDICK	Sir, I shall meet your wit in the career, an you charge it against me. I pray you choose another subject.
CLAUDIO	Nay, then, give him another staff: this last was broke cross. 135
DON PEDRO	By this light, he changes more and more. I think he be angry indeed.
CLAUDIO	If he be, he knows how to turn his girdle.
BENEDICK	Shall I speak a word in your ear? 140
CLAUDIO	God bless me from a challenge!

Don Pedro and Claudio
continue to try and joke with
Benedick. Benedick challenges
Claudio to a duel.

147 **so … cheer**: duelling was illegal, so
Claudio pretends that Benedick has
invited him to dinner

149–51 **calf … capon … woodcock**: all
considered stupid creatures

150 **curiously**: skilfully

151 **naught**: useless

152 **ambles well**: goes smoothly but with
no spirit

156 **gross**: coarse

158 **wise gentleman**: this is ironic

159 **hath the tongues**: is a master of
languages

160 **forswore**: took back

162 **trans-shape**: distort

164 **properest**: most handsome

Think about

• Don Pedro's light-hearted
remarks in lines 153 to 164
can seem out of place.
What evidence is there that
perhaps he has not heard
Benedick challenge
Claudio? Look at lines 148
and 184 to 187. How could
a director stage this?

• How might Benedick react
at this point to hearing
about Beatrice?

169–70 **God … garden**: a reference to:
1 Benedick hiding in Act 3 Scene 1;
2 God seeing Adam in the garden of
Eden

BENEDICK	(*Aside to* CLAUDIO) You are a villain. I jest not. I will make it good how you dare, with what you dare, and when you dare. Do me right, or I will protest your cowardice. You have killed a sweet lady, and her death shall fall heavy on you. Let me hear from you.

145

CLAUDIO	Well, I will meet you, so I may have good cheer.
DON PEDRO	What, a feast, a feast?
CLAUDIO	I' faith, I thank him. He hath bid me to a calf's head and a capon, the which if I do not carve most curiously, say my knife's naught. Shall I not find a woodcock too?

150

BENEDICK	Sir, your wit ambles well; it goes easily.
DON PEDRO	I'll tell thee how Beatrice praised *thy* wit the other day. I said, thou hadst a fine wit. 'True,' said she, 'a fine little one.' 'No,' said I, 'a great wit.' 'Right,' says she, 'a great gross one.' 'Nay,' said I, 'a good wit.' 'Just,' said she, 'it hurts nobody.' 'Nay,' said I, 'the gentleman is wise.' 'Certain,' said she, 'a wise gentleman.' 'Nay,' said I, 'he hath the tongues.' 'That I believe,' said she, 'for he swore a thing to me on Monday night which he forswore on Tuesday morning. There's a double tongue: there's two tongues.' Thus did she, an hour together, trans-shape thy particular virtues. Yet at last she concluded with a sigh, thou wast the properest man in Italy.

155

160

CLAUDIO	For the which she wept heartily, and said she cared not.

165

DON PEDRO	Yea, that she did. But yet, for all that, and if she did not hate him deadly, she would love him dearly. The old man's daughter told us all.
CLAUDIO	All, all – and, moreover, God saw him when he was hid in the garden.

170

DON PEDRO	But when shall we set the savage bull's horns on the sensible Benedick's head?
CLAUDIO	Yea, and text underneath: 'Here dwells Benedick, the married man'?

Claudio and Don Pedro are surprised at the change in Benedick. Dogberry and Verges bring in their prisoners, Borachio and Conrade.

176 **humour**: inclination
177 **braggarts**: boasters

182 **Lord Lack-beard**: another reference to Claudio's youth

189–90 **doublet and hose**: i.e. his clothes

191–2 **He ... man**: The fool may think that such a man is wise, but in fact the fool is much wiser than he is.
193 **soft you**: wait a minute
sad: serious

196 **ne'er ... balance**: never again weigh evidence in her scales

201 **Hearken after**: Enquire about

Think about

- Benedick calls Claudio 'Lord Lack-beard' (line 182). What do most of the insults aimed at Claudio have in common? Look back at Beatrice's, for example (Act 4 Scene 1, lines 307 to 312) and Leonato's (Act 5 Scene 1, lines 75 to 76 and 79).

- If you were the director, how would you have Don Pedro react to Benedick's parting speech?

BENEDICK	Fare you well, boy; you know my mind. I will leave you 175 now to your gossip-like humour. You break jests as braggarts do their blades, which, God be thanked, hurt not. (*To* DON PEDRO) My lord, for your many courtesies I thank you. I must discontinue your company. Your brother the bastard is fled from Messina. You have 180 among you killed a sweet and innocent lady. For my Lord Lack-beard there, he and I shall meet; and till then, peace be with him.

Exit.

DON PEDRO	He is in earnest.
CLAUDIO	In most profound earnest – and, I'll warrant you, for the 185 love of Beatrice.
DON PEDRO	And hath challenged thee.
CLAUDIO	Most sincerely.
DON PEDRO	What a pretty thing man is when he goes in his doublet and hose and leaves off his wit! 190
CLAUDIO	He is then a giant to an ape; but then is an ape a doctor to such a man.
DON PEDRO	But, soft you, let me be: pluck up, my heart, and be sad. Did he not say my brother was fled?

Enter DOGBERRY, VERGES, *and men of the Watch, with* CONRADE *and* BORACHIO *as prisoners.*

DOGBERRY	(*To* BORACHIO) Come, you, sir. If justice cannot tame 195 you, she shall ne'er weigh more reasons in her balance. Nay, an you be a cursing hypocrite once, you must be looked to.
DON PEDRO	How now, two of my brother's men bound? Borachio one! 200
CLAUDIO	Hearken after their offence, my lord.
DON PEDRO	Officers, what offence have these men done?

Borachio confesses his role in disgracing Hero. Claudio is overcome and very sorry.

206 **verified … things**: he possibly means 'testified', i.e. told lies

212 **division**: style
213 **one … suited**: one idea expressed in many ways

216 **cunning**: clever

Think about

• Borachio says that Don John asked him to slander Hero. Compare this with what actually happened in Act 2 Scene 2.

• Look at Borachio's explanation in lines 217 to 229. List some occasions in the play where people have (a) been deceived by what they see and (b) expressed the truth without realising it.

233 **practice**: doing

234 **composed and framed**: entirely made up

237 **semblance**: appearance

| DOGBERRY | Marry, sir, they have committed false report; moreover they have spoken untruths; secondarily, they are slanders; sixth and lastly, they have belied a lady; thirdly, they have verified unjust things; and to conclude, they are lying knaves. | 205 |

| DON PEDRO | First, I ask thee what they have done; thirdly, I ask thee what's their offence; sixth and lastly, why they are committed; and to conclude, what you lay to their charge. | 210 |

| CLAUDIO | Rightly reasoned, and in his own division. And, by my troth, there's one meaning well suited. | |

| DON PEDRO | Who have you offended, masters, that you are thus bound to your answer? This learnèd Constable is too cunning to be understood. What's your offence? | 215 |

| BORACHIO | Sweet Prince, let me go no farther to mine answer. Do you hear me, and let this Count kill me. I have deceived even your very eyes. What your wisdoms could not discover, these shallow fools have brought to light – who in the night overheard me confessing to this man how Don John your brother incensed me to slander the Lady Hero; how you were brought into the orchard and saw me court Margaret in Hero's garments; how you disgraced her, when you should marry her. My villainy they have upon record, which I had rather seal with my death than repeat over to my shame. The lady is dead upon mine and my master's false accusation. And briefly, I desire nothing but the reward of a villain. | 220

225 |

| DON PEDRO | Runs not this speech like iron through your blood? | 230 |

| CLAUDIO | I have drunk poison whiles he uttered it. | |

| DON PEDRO | But did my brother set thee on to this? | |

| BORACHIO | Yea, and paid me richly for the practice of it. | |

| DON PEDRO | He is composed and framed of treachery,
And fled he is upon this villainy. | 235 |

| CLAUDIO | Sweet Hero, now thy image doth appear
In the rare semblance that I loved it first. | |

Claudio and Don Pedro ask Leonato to punish them in whatever way he wishes. Leonato commands Claudio and Don Pedro to tell the people of Messina that Hero was innocent, and Claudio to compose a poem in her memory.

238 **plaintiffs**: he means the opposite, 'the defendants'

239 **reformed**: he means 'informed'

250 **beliest**: wrong

— **Think about** —

- Compare the remorse of the three wrong-doers, Borachio, Don Pedro and Claudio. Who takes the blame? What do the others say?

- Claudio's and Don Pedro's apologies in lines 256 to 263 often seem rather thin. How would you direct the actors to say them and Leonato to respond?

258 **Impose ... penance**: Make me suffer any punishment
invention: imagination

263 **enjoin me to**: impose on me

266 **Possess**: Inform

268 **aught**: in any way

269 **epitaph**: words about the dead person written on a tomb

DOGBERRY	Come, bring away the plaintiffs. By this time our Sexton hath reformed Signior Leonato of the matter. And, masters, do not forget to specify, when time and place 240 shall serve, that I am an ass.
VERGES	Here, here comes master Signior Leonato, and the Sexton too.

Enter LEONATO *and* ANTONIO, *with the* SEXTON.

LEONATO	Which is the villain? Let me see his eyes, That, when I note another man like him, 245 I may avoid him. Which of these is he?
BORACHIO	If you would know your wronger, look on me.
LEONATO	Art thou the slave that with thy breath hast killed Mine innocent child?
BORACHIO	Yea, even I alone.
LEONATO	No, not so, villain, thou beliest thyself – 250 Here stand a pair of honourable men, A third is fled, that had a hand in it. I thank you, Princes, for my daughter's death: Record it with your high and worthy deeds. 'Twas bravely done, if you bethink you of it. 255
CLAUDIO	I know not how to pray your patience, Yet I must speak. Choose your revenge yourself. Impose me to what penance your invention Can lay upon my sin. Yet sinned I not But in mistaking.
DON PEDRO	By my soul, nor I. 260 And yet, to satisfy this good old man, I would bend under any heavy weight That he'll enjoin me to.
LEONATO	I cannot bid you bid my daughter live: That were impossible. But I pray you both, 265 Possess the people in Messina here How innocent she died. And if your love Can labour aught in sad invention, Hang her an epitaph upon her tomb

Leonato commands Claudio to marry Antonio's daughter in place of Hero. Dogberry steps in and reminds Leonato that Conrade called him an ass.

276 Give … right: i.e. Marry her

279–80 dispose … Claudio: i.e. from now on I put myself entirely under your guidance

282 naughty: wicked

284 packed: involved

289–90 under … black: written down

294 borrows … name: i.e. begs

296 lend … sake: not give charity

Think about

• How would you respond to the suggestion that Claudio is being rewarded here rather than punished?

• Leonato invents another niece. Why does he do this?

300 youth: another of Dogberry's mistakes

301 pains: trouble

302 God … foundation: he is thanking Leonato as though he is receiving money from a charity

	And sing it to her bones: sing it tonight.	270
	Tomorrow morning come you to my house;	
	And since you could not be my son-in-law,	
	Be yet my nephew. My brother hath a daughter,	
	Almost the copy of my child that's dead;	
	And she alone is heir to both of us.	275
	Give her the right you should have given her cousin,	
	And so dies my revenge.	

CLAUDIO   O noble sir!
Your over-kindness doth wring tears from me.
I do embrace your offer – and dispose
For henceforth of poor Claudio.   280

LEONATO Tomorrow then I will expect your coming;
Tonight I take my leave. This naughty man
Shall face to face be brought to Margaret,
Who I believe was packed in all this wrong,
Hired to it by your brother.

BORACHIO   No, by my soul, she was not, 285
Nor knew not what she did when she spoke to me;
But always hath been just and virtuous
In anything that I do know by her.

DOGBERRY Moreover, sir, which indeed is not under white and
black, this plaintiff here, the offender, did call me ass. I 290
beseech you, let it be remembered in his punishment.
And also, the watch heard them talk of one Deformed:
they say he wears a key in his ear and a lock hanging by
it, and borrows money in God's name, the which he
hath used so long and never paid, that now men grow 295
hard-hearted and will lend nothing for God's sake. Pray
you, examine him upon that point.

LEONATO I thank thee for thy care and honest pains.

DOGBERRY Your worship speaks like a most thankful and reverend
youth, and I praise God for you.   300

LEONATO There's for thy pains. (*Gives him money*.)

DOGBERRY God save the foundation!

LEONATO Go; I discharge thee of thy prisoner, and I thank thee.

Dogberry leaves the prisoners with Leonato for him to punish. Leonato reminds Claudio and Don Pedro to meet the next day for Claudio's wedding.

304   **arrant**: total

309   **prohibit it**: he means the opposite, 'make it happen'

311   **look for**: will expect

314   **lewd**: base

Think about

• What is your final impression of Dogberry? Do you find him ridiculous or have you gained some affection or even sympathy for him?

• The scene ends with a reference to Margaret. In the Branagh film, Margaret is so guilty and frightened that she runs away from the wedding. How guilty is she, in your opinion?

DOGBERRY	I leave an arrant knave with your worship – which I beseech your worship to correct yourself, for the example of others. God keep your worship! I wish your worship well. God restore you to health! I humbly give you leave to depart; and if a merry meeting may be wished, God prohibit it! Come, neighbour.

305

Exit DOGBERRY, *with* VERGES.

LEONATO   Until tomorrow morning, lords, farewell.   310

ANTONIO   Farewell, my lords: we look for you tomorrow.

DON PEDRO   We will not fail.

CLAUDIO   Tonight I'll mourn with Hero.

Exit DON PEDRO, *with* CLAUDIO.

LEONATO   *(To the men of the Watch)*
Bring you these fellows on. We'll talk with Margaret,
How her acquaintance grew with this lewd fellow.

Exeunt.

In this scene ...

- Benedick tries to write a love poem for Beatrice.
- Benedick tells Beatrice that he has challenged Claudio.
- Ursula brings news of Hero's innocence and that Don John was responsible for what happened.

Benedick asks Margaret to fetch Beatrice. He tries to write a love poem.

5   **come over**: exceed
    comely: fair and proper (with a play on 'come over')

7   **below stairs**: i.e. in the servants' quarters

9   **foils**: light swords

12 **bucklers**: small, round shields

14 **pikes**: central spikes in shields

Think about

- The conversation between Benedick and Margaret is full of sexual innuendos (double meanings) including: 'come over' (have sex with), 'swords / pikes' and 'bucklers' (the male and female sex organs), and 'vice' (a woman's thighs). What effect does it have at this point in the play?

- Does Benedick's friendly conversation with Margaret make us feel more sympathetic towards her?

22–3 **Leander ... Troilus**: lovers from legend
23   **panders**: pimps
24–6 **quondam ... verse**: one-time ladies'-men (i.e. not soldiers) who are still remembered in poetry

Leonato's garden.

Enter BENEDICK *and* MARGARET.

BENEDICK	Pray thee, sweet Mistress Margaret, deserve well at my hands by helping me to the speech of Beatrice.
MARGARET	Will you then write me a sonnet in praise of my beauty?
BENEDICK	In so high a style, Margaret, that no man living shall come over it; for, in most comely truth, thou deservest it.
MARGARET	To have no man come over me! Why, shall I always keep below stairs?
BENEDICK	Thy wit is as quick as the greyhound's mouth: it catches.
MARGARET	And yours as blunt as the fencer's foils, which hit, but hurt not.
BENEDICK	A most manly wit, Margaret: it will not hurt a woman. And so, I pray thee, call Beatrice. I give thee the bucklers.
MARGARET	Give us the swords: we have bucklers of our own.
BENEDICK	If you use them, Margaret, you must put in the pikes with a vice – and they are dangerous weapons for maids.
MARGARET	Well, I will call Beatrice to you, who I think hath legs.

Exit.

BENEDICK   And therefore will come.
    (*Sings*)   'The God of love,
                That sits above,
                And knows me, and knows me,
                How pitiful I deserve –'

I mean in singing – but in loving, Leander the good swimmer, Troilus the first employer of panders, and a whole bookful of these quondam carpet-mongers, whose names yet run smoothly in the even road of a blank verse, why, they were never so truly turned over and over as my poor self in love. Marry, I cannot show it in rhyme. I have tried. I can find out no rhyme to 'lady'

Benedick tells Beatrice that he has challenged Claudio to a duel.

29 **innocent**: childish

32 **festival terms**: poetic language

37 **that I came**: what I came for

41 **noisome**: nasty

45 **undergoes**: i.e. has accepted (and now has to show up)

46 **subscribe**: announce

49 **politic**: well-organized

53 **epithet**: expression

Think about

• What is the tone of the banter between Beatrice and Benedick in this scene? How does it differ in tone from their earlier exchanges (especially Act 1 Scene 1 and Act 2 Scene1)?

• What might we work out from the fact that Benedick uses the 'thou' form and Beatrice the more polite 'you' form throughout this scene?

but 'baby' – an innocent rhyme; for 'scorn', 'horn' – a hard rhyme; for 'school', 'fool' – a babbling rhyme: very ominous endings. No, I was not born under a rhyming planet, nor I cannot woo in festival terms. **30**

Enter BEATRICE.

Sweet Beatrice, would'st thou come when I called thee?

BEATRICE	Yea, signior, and depart when you bid me.
BENEDICK	O, stay but till then! **35**
BEATRICE	'Then' is spoken: fare you well now. And yet, ere I go, let me go with that I came – which is, with knowing what hath passed between you and Claudio.
BENEDICK	Only foul words: and thereupon I will kiss thee.
BEATRICE	Foul words is but foul wind, and foul wind is but foul **40** breath, and foul breath is noisome: therefore I will depart unkissed.
BENEDICK	Thou hast frighted the word out of his right sense, so forcible is thy wit. But I must tell thee plainly, Claudio undergoes my challenge; and either I must shortly hear **45** from him, or I will subscribe him a coward. And I pray thee now, tell me for which of my bad parts didst thou first fall in love with me?
BEATRICE	For them all together; which maintained so politic a state of evil that they will not admit any good part to **50** intermingle with them. But for which of my good parts did you first suffer love for me?
BENEDICK	'Suffer love!' – a good epithet. I do suffer love indeed, for I love thee against my will.
BEATRICE	In spite of your heart, I think. Alas, poor heart! If you **55** spite it for my sake, I will spite it for yours: for I will never love that which my friend hates.
BENEDICK	Thou and I are too wise to woo peaceably.
BEATRICE	It appears not in this confession. There's not one wise man among twenty that will praise himself. **60**

Ursula brings news that Hero has been proved innocent.

61 **instance**: saying

61–2 **time … neighbours**: old days

63–4 **live ... than**: have no memorial longer than

66 **Question**: A good question
clamour: tolling the funeral bell

67 **rheum**: tears

68 **Don Worm**: 'Sir Worm' – referring to the popular idea of conscience gnawing like a worm

78 **old coil**: a great to-do

80 **abused**: deceived

82 **presently**: immediately

84 **die in thy lap**: can mean 'have sex with you'

Think about

- Unlike most other male characters, Benedick shows real concern for Hero (lines 71 to 72). In what ways has Benedick changed since the beginning of the play?

- Benedick's 'die in thy lap' (line 84) can also mean 'have sex with you'. Is this too bold of Benedick at this point?

BENEDICK	An old, an old instance, Beatrice – that lived in the time of good neighbours. If a man do not erect in this age his own tomb ere he dies, he shall live no longer in monument than the bell rings and the widow weeps.
BEATRICE	And how long is that, think you?
BENEDICK	Question – why, an hour in clamour and a quarter in rheum. Therefore is it most expedient for the wise, if Don Worm, his conscience, find no impediment to the contrary, to be the trumpet of his own virtues, as I am to myself. So much for praising myself, who, I myself will bear witness, is praiseworthy. And now tell me, how doth your cousin?
BEATRICE	Very ill.
BENEDICK	And how do you?
BEATRICE	Very ill too.
BENEDICK	Serve God, love me, and mend. There will I leave you too, for here comes one in haste.

Enter URSULA.

URSULA	Madam, you must come to your uncle. Yonder's old coil at home. It is proved my Lady Hero hath been falsely accused, the Prince and Claudio mightily abused, and Don John is the author of all, who is fled and gone. Will you come presently?
BEATRICE	Will you go hear this news, signior?
BENEDICK	I will live in thy heart, die in thy lap and be buried in thy eyes. And moreover, I will go with thee to thy uncle's.

Exeunt.

65

70

75

80

85

In this scene ...

- Claudio mourns at Hero's tomb.
- Claudio and Don Pedro depart to prepare for Claudio's wedding.

Claudio hangs a poem on Hero's tomb in her memory and Balthasar sings a funeral song.

5   **guerdon**: compensation

12   **goddess of the night**: Diana

Think about

- This scene takes place at Hero's monument. It opens at night, but dawn is approaching by the end. How would you stage this?

18   **Heavily**: Mournfully

20   **utterèd**: fully expressed

The church: near Leonato's family monument.

Enter CLAUDIO, DON PEDRO, BALTHASAR *with musicians, and*

three or four gentlemen carrying candles, all wearing

mourning clothes.

CLAUDIO	Is this the monument of Leonato?
A GENTLEMAN	It is, my lord.

CLAUDIO   (*Reading Hero's epitaph from a scroll*)
Done to death by slanderous tongues
  Was the Hero that here lies.
Death, in guerdon of her wrongs,   5
  Gives her fame which never dies.
So the life that died with shame
  Lives in death with glorious fame.
Hang thou there upon the tomb,
                    (*Hanging the scroll on the tomb*)
  Praising her when I am dumb.   10
Now, music, sound; and sing your solemn hymn.

BALTHASAR

  Song

          Pardon, goddess of the night,
          Those that slew thy virgin knight;
          For the which, with songs of woe,
          Round about her tomb they go.   15
          Midnight, assist our moan,
          Help us to sigh and groan,
            Heavily, heavily.
          Graves yawn and yield your dead,
          Till death be utterèd,   20
            Heavily, heavily.

CLAUDIO   Now, unto thy bones good night.
          Yearly will I do this rite.

Don Pedro and Claudio set off to Leonato's house for the wedding.

26 wheels of Phoebus: i.e. the sun

29 several: own

30 weeds: clothes

32 Hymen: god of marriage
speed's: favour us

Think about

- Apart from the songs, there is very little rhyme in this play. But, after the rhyming epitaph and song, Don Pedro and Claudio continue to speak in rhyme. What effect does this have?

DON PEDRO	Good morrow, masters. Put your torches out.
	The wolves have preyed, and look, the gentle day, **25**
	Before the wheels of Phoebus, round about
	Dapples the drowsy east with spots of grey.
	Thanks to you all, and leave us. Fare you well.
CLAUDIO	Good morrow, masters: each his several way.
DON PEDRO	Come, let us hence, and put on other weeds; **30**
	And then to Leonato's we will go.
CLAUDIO	And Hymen now with luckier issue speed's
	Than this for whom we rendered up this woe.

Exeunt.

195

In this scene ...

- Everyone gathers for the second wedding.
- Benedick states his desire to marry Beatrice.
- Hero is revealed to be alive. She and Claudio are reunited.
- Beatrice and Benedick publicly declare their affection for one another.
- A messenger arrives with news that Don John has been captured.

There is general joy that Hero's name has been cleared. Leonato sends the women to put on masks. Benedick asks Leonato for permission to marry Beatrice.

3 **debated**: explained

5 **against her will**: unintentionally

6 **question**: investigation

7 **sort**: turn out

8 **by faith**: i.e. he gave his word to Beatrice

14 **office**: job

17 **confirmed countenance**: straight face

18 **pains**: help

20 **undo**: ruin

24 **requite her**: return her feelings

---**Think about**---

- How do you react to Leonato's comment that Don Pedro and Claudio are 'innocent' whereas Margaret 'was in some fault for this' (lines 2 to 4)? Is that your view too?

At Leonato's house.

Enter Leonato, Antonio, Benedick, Beatrice, Margaret, Ursula, Friar Francis *and* Hero.

Friar Did I not tell you she was innocent?

Leonato So are the Prince and Claudio, who accused her
Upon the error that you heard debated.
But Margaret was in some fault for this,
Although against her will, as it appears
In the true course of all the question.

Antonio Well, I am glad that all things sort so well.

Benedick And so am I, being else by faith enforced
To call young Claudio to a reckoning for it.

Leonato Well, daughter, and you gentlewomen all,
Withdraw into a chamber by yourselves;
And when I send for you, come hither masked.
The Prince and Claudio promised by this hour
To visit me. You know your office, brother:
You must be father to your brother's daughter,
And give her to young Claudio.

Exit Hero, *with* Beatrice, Margaret *and* Ursula.

Antonio Which I will do with confirmed countenance.

Benedick Friar, I must entreat your pains, I think.

Friar To do what, signior?

Benedick To bind me, or undo me – one of them.
Signior Leonato: truth it is, good signior,
Your niece regards me with an eye of favour.

Leonato That eye my daughter lent her. 'Tis most true.

Benedick And I do with an eye of love requite her.

Leonato The sight whereof I think you had from me,
From Claudio, and the Prince. But what's your will?

Claudio arrives, believing that he is about to marry Antonio's daughter. Claudio and Don Pedro tease Benedick about his change of heart.

Think about

- Claudio's reply in line 38 is racist. In a recent production, Margaret was played by a black actress who remained on stage and reacted angrily. How would you deal with the line in a production?

- According to Don Pedro, Benedick has 'a February face' (line 41), meaning that he looks cold and unwelcoming. Is Benedick friends with Claudio again, or is he still angry with him? What does their exchange in lines 43 to 52 suggest? Look at the use of 'thou' and 'you'.

---

27 **enigmatical**: puzzling / mysterious

36 **yet**: still

38 **Ethiope**: in Shakespeare's time this was a term for any black African

44 **tip ... gold**: make you a fine cuckold
45 **Europa**: Europe
46 **Europa**: a princess, carried off by Jupiter in the form of a bull

48 **amiable low**: pleasing voice

50 **got**: fathered

52 **owe you**: will be even with you
    other reckonings: other accounts I must settle first

BENEDICK	Your answer, sir, is enigmatical.
	But, for my will, my will is your good will
	May stand with ours, this day to be conjoined
	In the state of honourable marriage –
	In which, good Friar, I shall desire your help.

30

LEONATO	My heart is with your liking.
FRIAR	And my help.
	Here comes the Prince and Claudio.

Enter DON PEDRO *and* CLAUDIO, *with attendants.*

DON PEDRO	Good morrow to this fair assembly.
LEONATO	Good morrow, Prince; good morrow, Claudio.

35

	We here attend you. Are you yet determined
	Today to marry with my brother's daughter?
CLAUDIO	I'll hold my mind, were she an Ethiope.
LEONATO	Call her forth, brother; here's the Friar ready.

Exit ANTONIO.

DON PEDRO	Good morrow, Benedick. Why, what's the matter,

40

	That you have such a February face,
	So full of frost, of storm and cloudiness?
CLAUDIO	I think he thinks upon the savage bull.
	Tush, fear not, man, we'll tip thy horns with gold,
	And all Europa shall rejoice at thee,

45

	As once Europa did at lusty Jove,
	When he would play the noble beast in love.
BENEDICK	Bull Jove, sir, had an amiable low –
	And some such strange bull leaped your father's cow,
	And got a calf in that same noble feat

50

	Much like to you, for you have just his bleat.
CLAUDIO	For this I owe you. Here comes other reckonings.

Enter ANTONIO, *with* HERO, BEATRICE, MARGARET *and* URSULA, *wearing masks.*

	Which is the lady I must seize upon?
ANTONIO	This same is she, and I do give you her.

At the wedding Claudio is amazed to discover that his bride is actually Hero. Beatrice and Benedick deny that they ever loved each other.

63 defiled: i.e. disgraced
64 maid: virgin

67 qualify: 1 moderate; 2 explain away

69 largely: in full detail
70 let ... familiar: treat this amazing event as an ordinary occurrence
71 presently: immediately
72 Soft and fair: i.e. Just a minute

Think about

• This is Hero's first appearance since her supposed death. Does she seem to be changed in any way?

• How do you imagine Hero is feeling at this time?

• How would you direct an actress to play her speeches with Claudio?

---

81 well-nigh: almost

CLAUDIO	Why, then she's mine. Sweet, let me see your face.	**55**
ANTONIO	No, that you shall not, till you take her hand Before this Friar, and swear to marry her.	
CLAUDIO	Give me your hand: before this holy Friar, I am your husband, if you like of me.	
HERO	(*Unmasking*) And when I lived, I was your other wife; And when you loved, you were my other husband.	**60**
CLAUDIO	Another Hero!	
HERO	Nothing certainer. One Hero died defiled, but I do live; And surely as I live I am a maid.	
DON PEDRO	The former Hero! Hero that is dead!	**65**
LEONATO	She died, my lord, but whiles her slander lived.	
FRIAR	All this amazement can I qualify, When, after that the holy rites are ended, I'll tell you largely of fair Hero's death. Meantime let wonder seem familiar, And to the chapel let us presently.	**70**
BENEDICK	Soft and fair, Friar. Which is Beatrice?	
BEATRICE	(*Unmasking*) I answer to that name. What is your will?	
BENEDICK	Do not you love me?	
BEATRICE	Why no – no more than reason.	
BENEDICK	Why, then your uncle and the Prince and Claudio Have been deceived. They swore you did.	**75**
BEATRICE	Do not you love me?	
BENEDICK	Troth, no – no more than reason.	
BEATRICE	Why, then my cousin, Margaret and Ursula Are much deceived: for they did swear you did.	
BENEDICK	They swore that you were almost sick for me.	**80**
BEATRICE	They swore that you were well-nigh dead for me.	
BENEDICK	'Tis no such matter. Then you do not love me?	

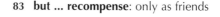

Claudio and Hero produce love
poems written by Beatrice and
Benedick proving their love for
one another.

83 **but ... recompense**: only as friends

87 **halting**: lamely written

96 **in a consumption**: i.e. dying for love of
me

100 **flout**: mock
101 **care for**: am hurt by
satire ... epigram: i.e. empty mocking
words
103 **purpose**: intend

106 **giddy**: changeable

111 **cudgelled**: beaten
112 **double-dealer**: 1 someone who has a
partner; 2 deceiver
113–14 **look ... to**: keep a close eye on

Think about

• What is Claudio implying
about Benedick in lines 110
to 114?

• How do you think Benedick
should say 'Come, come,
we are friends' (line 115)?

BEATRICE	No, truly, but in friendly recompense.
LEONATO	Come, cousin, I am sure you love the gentleman.
CLAUDIO	And I'll be sworn upon't that he loves her; 85 For here's a paper written in his hand, A halting sonnet of his own pure brain, Fashioned to Beatrice.
HERO	And here's another, Writ in my cousin's hand, stolen from her pocket, Containing her affection unto Benedick. 90
BENEDICK	A miracle! Here's our own hands against our hearts. Come, I will have thee: but, by this light, I take thee for pity.
BEATRICE	I would not deny you; but, by this good day, I yield upon great persuasion – and partly to save your life, 95 for I was told you were in a consumption.
BENEDICK	Peace! I will stop your mouth. (***Kissing her***)
DON PEDRO	How dost thou, Benedick the married man?
BENEDICK	I'll tell thee what, Prince. A college of wit-crackers cannot flout me out of my humour. Dost thou think I 100 care for a satire or an epigram? No: if a man will be beaten with brains, 'a shall wear nothing handsome about him. In brief, since I do purpose to marry, I will think nothing to any purpose that the world can say against it. And therefore never flout at me for what I 105 have said against it – for man is a giddy thing, and this is my conclusion. For thy part, Claudio, I did think to have beaten thee: but in that thou art like to be my kinsman, live unbruised, and love my cousin.
CLAUDIO	I had well hoped, thou wouldst have denied Beatrice, 110 that I might have cudgelled thee out of thy single life, to make thee a double-dealer – which out of question thou wilt be, if my cousin do not look exceeding narrowly to thee.
BENEDICK	Come, come, we are friends. Let's have a dance ere 115 we are married, that we may lighten our own hearts and our wives' heels.

Benedick proposes a dance
before the wedding ceremony. A
messenger brings word that Don
John has been arrested. He will
be punished after the weddings
have taken place.

120–1 There ... horn: a last cuckold joke

124 brave: great

---Think about ---

In one production, Beatrice
and Benedick carried on
arguing during the dance
which ends the play and
didn't notice that the other
characters had left.
• How would you end the
  play?

• Would you highlight the
  fact that Don Pedro is left
  without a partner?

LEONATO   We'll have dancing afterward.

BENEDICK   First, of my word! Therefore play, music. Prince, thou
            art sad: get thee a wife, get thee a wife! There is no 120
            staff more reverend than one tipped with horn.

       Enter a MESSENGER.

MESSENGER   My lord, your brother John is ta'en in flight,
            And brought with armed men back to Messina.

BENEDICK   Think not on him till tomorrow. I'll devise thee brave
            punishments for him. Strike up, pipers!   125

                                                            Dance.

                                                            Exeunt.

RSC, 1982

Renaissance Films, 1993

RSC, 1986

Open Air Theatre, Regent's Park, 2000

RSC, 1982

RSC,2002

Much Ado About Nothing is a comedy about love and deception. It takes place in Messina, Italy, and revolves around a funny and high-spirited group of people – in particular, Beatrice and Benedick. These two characters are the stars of the play, even though many of the dramatic events centre around the young lovers Hero and Claudio. During Shakespeare's lifetime the play was sometimes referred to as 'Beatrice and Benedick'.

COMEDY

Shakespeare's comedies focus on the lighter aspects of life and often include dances and songs. Villains and mischievous schemes feature in them, but there are no real tragedies or deaths, and the plot moves towards a happy ending. Unlike the tragedies they begin with chaos and end in order. They centre on love and courtship and usually end with a wedding about to take place. In all the comedies, the women are wiser than the men about the nature of love and relationships. The men have to grow up and learn the meaning of true love. The comedies also contain humorous, often lower-class, characters such as Dogberry, the bungling town constable, who misuses important-sounding words with comic effect.

LOVE AND COURTSHIP

In Shakespeare's time it was common for marriage to be as much about money and social connections as love. Marriages were often, for example, arranged by the fathers, rather than the couples themselves, especially among the wealthier classes. In *Much Ado About Nothing*, the two couples show two different attitudes towards courtship, the ritual that leads towards marriage. The courtship of one couple is very traditional, whilst the other seems less conventional and perhaps more modern.

When the young Claudio falls in love with Hero, he also asks Don Pedro (his commanding officer) whether Leonato has any other children. He wants to know whether Hero will inherit all her father's wealth. Since Don Pedro is a powerful and important figure, he offers to speak to Leonato and Hero on Claudio's behalf. In fact, Claudio and Hero hardly ever speak to each other in the play and are never alone together. With Beatrice and Benedick, however, it is different. They have known each other for some time, and once they have realized that they are in love, they speak to each other openly about it. Their relationship is founded on love and trust, even though they continue to argue. Even Benedick, though, follows the rules. He asks Leonato, Beatrice's guardian, for his permission to marry her.

HONOUR

Messina is a male-dominated society, like Shakespearean England. The idea of honour, or reputation, was different for men and women. For men it was based on family, class and reputation among other men. For women it depended on being sexually pure. Men could defend their honour by challenging another man to a duel, but this option was not open to women – they had to depend upon men to uphold their honour for them. Hero's honour is challenged by Claudio when he accuses her of being unfaithful. Leonato, her father, does not immediately try to defend her because he is more concerned about his status as father and dignity among the other men. Honour would come to Leonato if his daughter married a friend of the Prince, Don Pedro, the character with the highest status in the play.

THE VILLAIN

The comedies usually contain a character or situation that threatens the happiness of the lovers. In *Much Ado About Nothing*, this takes the shape of the spiteful Don John. Don John is a *malcontent*: he makes trouble even when there is nothing to gain by it. He is an illegitimate son (the stage directions call him the 'Bastard'). Shakespeare's audiences would have understood the anger of illegitimate sons who would not inherit their fathers' lands or titles. Because this is a comedy, however, Don John does not finally triumph. He is arrested before he can do any real harm and he is missing from the happy ending.

GETTING TO KNOW THE CHARACTERS

It is important to get to know the characters and their relationships with each other, e.g. daughter, niece. Below is a range of games you can play at the beginning of lessons to help you do that. They can be played individually or in teams and you don't have to play all of them. Each one is more difficult than the previous one.

Before you play any of the games, you will need to read the outline of the plot and the character overview on pages 2 to 7. You will also need to make cards for the following characters: Leonato, Antonio, Don Pedro, Claudio, Benedick, Don John, Hero, Beatrice, Margaret and Dogberry.

- Colour-code your cards by choosing a colour that is appropriate, e.g. black for Don John.

- Group the characters by colour, e.g. use the same colour for Leonato and Antonio.

GAME 1
Set your chairs into a circle. Get into teams of three or four, each with a character card.

- One person reads out the outline of the plot on pages 2 to 5, or the summaries at the beginning of each scene.

- When your team's character is mentioned, one of your team moves into the centre of the circle, holding the character card. The team member remains in the circle until it is clear from the plot summary that the character exits, or until the beginning of the next scene.

GAME 2
Place your cards in the centre of the group facing upwards so you can see all the names.

- Player 1 picks up a card, says something about that character and puts it down.
  Player 1: Hero – I am the cousin of Beatrice.

- Player 2 picks up a card, says something about the character and puts it down, and so on.
  Player 2: Leonato – I am the governor of Messina.

- If a player picks up a card that has been used before they must say something new about the character.

GAME 3

Place your cards in the centre of the group facing downwards so you can't see the names.

- Player 1 picks up a card, shows it to the group, says something about the character and then puts the card down.
  Player 1 turns over the card of Don John: I am the brother of Don Pedro.

- Player 2 picks up a card, says something about the character and so on.
  Player 2 turns over the card of Beatrice: I am the niece of Leonato.

GAME 4

Place the cards face upwards in the centre so you can see all the names.

- Player 1 picks up a card and describes the relationship the character has with another character but without revealing their name.
  Player 1: I am Hero and I am the cousin of ...
  Player 2: Beatrice.

- Player 2 decides which character this is and picks up that character's card. Then Player 2 describes a relationship that character has with another character without revealing their name.
  Player 2: I was brought up by my uncle ...

- Player 3 decides which character this is and does the same as Player 2.
  Player 3: Leonato ...

GAME 5

Place the cards face downwards in the centre so you can't see the names.

- Player 1 picks up a card without letting the other players see the name. Player 1 gives a clue to the character's identity. Whoever guesses the identity of the character becomes Player 2.
  Player 1: I have taken a fancy to Leonato's daughter.
  Player 2: Claudio

- Player 2 picks up a card without revealing the character's name and does as Player 1 did.
  Player 2: I am an independent and stubborn woman.

GAME 6

Place the cards face upwards so you can see all the names.

- Without picking up a card Player 1 says which character they have chosen. Then Player 1 picks up two cards, one for a character their character likes and one for a character their character does not like. Finally they state their reasons.
  Player 1: I am Beatrice.
  Player 1 picks up the cards for Hero and Claudio: I like Hero because she has been a good friend to me since we were very young. I do not like Claudio because he shamed Hero in the church.

- Player 2 decides to be one of the characters that Player 1 picked up. Player 2 picks up two character cards, one that their character likes and one that their character does not like, and so on.

GAME 7

Place the cards face upwards so you can see all the names.

- Players 1 and 2 pick up a card each and become the characters they have chosen. They begin a short improvisation based on the play. Player 1 speaks first and the scene should end when one of the characters has a reason to leave.
  Player 1 picks up the card for Hero. Player 2 picks up the card for Beatrice. The two players begin a scene in which Hero is asking Beatrice to help her get dressed for her wedding. The scene could end with Beatrice leaving to see if the men are coming.
  Player 1: Beatrice, help me place these flowers in my hair.

- The next two players pick up character cards and begin an improvisation based on the play, and so on.

GAME 8

Place your cards in the centre of the group facing downwards so you can't see the names.

- Player 1 picks up a card, states the name of the character and gives three important actions they perform in the play.
  Player 1: I am Claudio. I fall in love with Hero. I shame Hero at the church. I marry Hero when I find she is alive.

- Player 2 picks up a card, states the name of the character and gives three important actions they perform in the play, and so on.
  Player 2: I am Leonato …

GETTING TO KNOW THE PLAY

This activity explores some of the major themes in the play: love, marriage, self-deception and the different roles of men and women. It can be used when you have just started reading the play or when you have been studying the play for some time.

Before you do this activity, you may need to read the outline of the plot on pages 2 to 5 or the summaries at the beginning of each scene. You are going to take part in a TV show about Beatrice and Benedick called 'This is Your Life'. It is going to involve:

- making a book about Beatrice's life and a book about Benedick's life

- writing dialogue between the presenter and different guests that know Beatrice and Benedick.

1   Divide into two large groups: one group to work on the book for Beatrice, and one group to work on the book for Benedick. Then divide into pairs to work on one of the sections below from the book you are working on. Each book will be divided into the seven sections below.

BEATRICE – THIS IS YOUR LIFE	BENEDICK – THIS IS YOUR LIFE
Childhood in Messina	Childhood
Early relationship with Benedick	Girlfriends – earlier visits to Messina
Friends starting to get married	Joining the army / Meeting Claudio
Sparring with Benedick	Sparring with Beatrice
The trick played on you by Claudio and Leonato	The trick played on you by Don Pedro, Hero and Ursula
The shaming of Hero	The challenge to Claudio
The forthcoming marriage to Benedick	The forthcoming marriage to Beatrice

2 **a** In your pairs choose two guests who will talk to the presenter about your section of the book.

   b Write the dialogue between the presenter and two guests who will be introduced in your section of the book. (You may also need to collect some items for your section of the book, e.g. drawings, letters, small objects.)

   Example

   Beatrice's childhood in Messina

   Presenter: After Beatrice's parents died when she was three, she went to live with her Uncle Leonato and grew up with Hero as almost a sister.

   Leonato could tell the story of how he took her in and how mischievous she was as a toddler.

   Hero could talk about their close friendship and of the games they played at Beatrice's suggestion.

3 Once your books are completed, clip each section together in order. Now they can be presented as a television show. Decide who will take the following roles:

   - the presenter of the show
   - the guests in each section of the story (e.g. the pair who worked on Beatrice's childhood would take the roles of Leonato and Hero)
   - other on-set characters: make-up artists, cameramen, wardrobe assistants.

4 Write an article about Benedick and Beatrice for a magazine or paper of your choice. You could include the writers of these articles in your 'This is Your Life' show.

   Examples

   - **Write as a journalist revealing a secret lonely-hearts ad written by Beatrice when she was 13.**
   - **Write as a psychologist speculating on the likely happiness of the Beatrice–Benedick marriage.**
   - **Write as a journalist from *Hello* magazine with an exclusive on the wedding for next month's issue.**

The activities in this section focus on different scenes in the play. The type of activities used can easily be adapted to focus on other sections of the play if necessary. Before beginning the activities you will need to have read the relevant scene.

ACT 2 SCENE 1: THE MASKED BALL

Each activity in this section leads directly onto the next. However, it is possible to use any of them separately. The focus of the activities is on the nature of love and courtship.

THE MASKED DANCE: THE GAME OF LOVE

As the soldiers enter Leonato's great hall wearing masks, the musicians start to play and the ball begins. As everyone dances, the audience hears snippets of conversation from four of the dancing couples.

1   In pairs, work on one of the four conversations below. Read through the section you have chosen.

- Don Pedro and Hero (lines 73 to 83)
- Balthasar and Margaret (lines 84 to 94)
- Ursula and Antonio (lines 95 to 105)
- Beatrice and Benedick (lines 106 to 132)

2   a   Each of the conversations listed above has a different 'flavour'. With your partner discuss the style and content of your section.
        Example
        Don Pedro and Hero's conversation takes the form of serious courtship. The style is formal with Don Pedro taking the lead. The content is almost entirely partnership, attraction and even love.

    b   When you have discussed this, come up with a freeze-frame (a still picture) of the two characters that captures the feeling between them. Imagine that a photographer from a newspaper has taken an interesting photo of them.

217

3 a Divide into groups of three. Decide who will take the roles of the couples listed in activity 1, e.g. Don Pedro and Hero. The other person will be a reporter.

b The couple should now work through their part of the scene, reading the lines and adding in suitable movement.

While they are doing this, the person playing the reporter should work on a gossipy account of the lovers' conversation. The reporter should decide what a journalist might think about their conversation.

Example:

A columnist overhearing Don Pedro and Hero's conversation would think Don Pedro wanted Hero for himself. This would be big news.

c Choose four groups that each worked on a different couple listed in activity 1. Each group is going to perform their conversation and journalist's report of it in front of the class. Create a small space that can be the 'dance-floor' with a place for the reporter to hide – perhaps under a table.

d The couple from the first group, e.g. Don Pedro and Hero, should act out their conversation. The reporter should come out of hiding and then give a gossipy account of their conversation to the audience. Finally the group should show the freeze-frame they worked on, which is the reporter's exclusive snapshot of the couple.

4 As a group, discuss the effect of masks being worn during this dance. You could consider:

- the effect of masks being worn at such dances
- the effect of masks being worn in this scene
- whether or not any of the couples are deceived, or if they know who they are dancing with
- if you think wearing masks allows some of the characters to be more honest than they might otherwise be.

CLAUDIO

Straight after the dance, Don John practises a sinister version of the deception game on Claudio. He pretends that he thinks Claudio is Benedick and tells Claudio that Don Pedro is wooing Hero for himself. Claudio's reaction to this 'trick' has important repercussions through the play.

1 In pairs improvise a short scene with one of you playing Don John and the other playing Claudio. The scene should begin with Don John approaching Claudio and telling him that he is certain that Don Pedro wishes to marry Hero. You should focus on the way we would expect Claudio to react rather than the way he reacts in the play.

Consider:
- what you expect Claudio's reaction will be, considering that Don Pedro is a trusted friend
- whether you expect Claudio to believe what Don John tells him, considering that he is known to be a villain.

2 Read lines 147 to 157, where we hear Claudio's actual reaction to what Don John has told him.

As a group, discuss the character of Claudio:
- What do you think is important to Claudio?
- How would you describe his relationships with Benedick and Don Pedro?
- How old would you like the actor playing Claudio to be, and why?
- What effect do you think Claudio's gullibility has on this joyful scene?
- Why do you think Claudio trusts Don John later in the play even though he is a liar? What does this say about Claudio's character?

HERO

Hero hardly speaks during this scene, apart from the short conversation she has with Don Pedro while she is dancing with him. We are not shown how she feels, for example, about being wooed by one man and then given to his friend.

1 The following are points in the scene where we might expect Hero to speak but she does not. In pairs one person should speak the line from the text. The other person should say what Hero might be thinking. Think about what she might have said if she had replied.

- Near the beginning of the scene, after Beatrice has said that she won't be married (lines 43 to 44).

  ANTONIO   (*To* HERO) Well, niece, I trust you will be ruled by your father.

  Consider whether Hero is happy to marry who her father chooses.

- In the middle of the scene, when Don Pedro is telling Benedick that he was wooing Hero on behalf of Claudio (lines 202 to 203).

  DON PEDRO   I will but teach them to sing, and restore them to the owner.

  Consider how Hero feels about being treated as a possession.

- Towards the end of the scene when, after a prompt from Beatrice, Claudio finally proposes to Hero (lines 270 to 272).

  CLAUDIO   Lady, as you are mine, I am yours: I give away myself for you and dote upon the exchange.

  Consider why Hero does not reply to this. All day she has been primed to think of Don Pedro as her future husband. How does she feel about marrying Claudio instead? Does she feel that it was cruel of Don Pedro to woo her for someone else?

BEATRICE AND BENEDICK

There are lots of hidden references in this scene to how Beatrice and Benedick feel about the state of marriage and about each other. These snippets of their ongoing story seem to hold the scene together.

1   In groups of three, read through the following sections:

  • Beatrice saying she will never marry (lines 13 to 42)
  • Beatrice and Benedick's conversation when dancing (lines 106 to 132)
  • Benedick's speeches and his exit (lines 185 to 195, 209 to 229, and 231 to 242)
  • Beatrice's speech hinting at a past relationship with Benedick (lines 245 to 248)
  • Don Pedro's plan to get Beatrice and Benedick together (lines 317 to 340)

2   **a**   In groups of three construct a 10-line scene from the above sections that shows the story of Beatrice and Benedick through the scene. You can use lines straight from the text or more modern language.

  b   Act out your scene with one actor taking the role of Beatrice, one taking the role of Benedick and the third taking the role of a director. In addition, the third person should play any other characters that you have included in your scene. The director should:

  • suggest where the actors move in the scene
  • suggest what emotions each character should be feeling and make sure that these are revealed by body language, facial expression and tone of voice.

3   In groups discuss the relationship between Beatrice and Benedick from what we have seen so far. Do you expect Don Pedro's plan to bring them together to work?

ACT 2 SCENE 3 AND ACT 3 SCENE 1: THE GARDEN SCENES

Each activity in this section leads directly onto the next. However, it is possible to use any of them separately. The focus of the activities is on deception.

THE GAME OF DECEPTION

1   The tricksters use examples that they think will persuade Beatrice that Benedick is in love with her and vice versa. For example, Leonato says that Beatrice is up twenty times a night trying to write to Benedick.

   a   Imagine you are Leonato and think about the traditional behaviour expected of lovers. Make a list of all the things Hero might have 'seen' Beatrice do that would convince the listener (Benedick) that she was lovestruck.
   Examples
   • Calling his name in her sleep
   • Embroidering his initials onto her handkerchief

   b   Imagine you are Hero. Compile a similar list of things which Claudio might have 'seen' Benedick do.
   Examples
   • Composing a song about her
   • Buying new fashionable clothes he thinks she will like

2   Another part of the trick might have been to drop a letter which Beatrice/Benedick was supposed to have written to the other. Write the two letters below in modern language. Try to include a few of Beatrice/Benedick's sayings or try to capture something of the way they speak so that the letters could believably have been written by Beatrice/Benedick.

   a   Imagine you are Leonato and Don Pedro. Write a letter that pretends to be from Benedick to Beatrice.

   b   Imagine you are Hero and Ursula. Write a letter that pretends to be from Beatrice to Benedick.

THE DARKER SIDE OF DECEPTION: HARSH CRITICISMS

In Act 2 Scene 3 Don Pedro and the others speak critically of Benedick. For example, Don Pedro says that Benedick has 'a contemptible spirit'. In Act 3 Scene 1 Hero is even more harsh in her criticism of Beatrice.

1 In a stage production we are very conscious of the effect that the critical words about Beatrice and Benedick are having on them as they hide.

   a In pairs one person should look at Act 2 Scene 3 and the other at Act 3 Scene 1. Go through the text and make a list of all the insults that are used against Benedick and Beatrice. You can write these in the Shakespearean language or in modern language.

   b Now take on the roles of Don Pedro and Benedick. Using the list of insults against Benedick, the person playing Don Pedro should speak the insults. The person playing Benedick should listen to the criticisms of his character from his hiding place. After each insult is read out Benedick should respond by revealing what he is thinking and feeling.
   Example: Act 2 Scene 3, lines 148–9

   CLAUDIO   To what end? He would make but a sport of it, and torment the poor lady worse.

   Benedick's response: I would not! My intention was never to torment her!

   c Now take on the roles of Hero and Beatrice. Using the list of insults against Beatrice, the person playing Hero should speak the insult. The person playing Beatrice should respond to each criticism by saying what she is thinking and feeling.
   Example: Act 3 Scene 1, line 74

   HERO   But who dare tell her so?

   Beatrice's response: Are people really scared to tell me the truth? Is my best friend frightened to tell me what she really thinks?

2 a In pairs think of three emotions that Benedick may be feeling when he is finally alone in Act 2 Scene 3.

   b Now do the same for when Beatrice is finally alone in Act 3 Scene 1.

SETTING UP THE SHAMING OF HERO

In many ways the deceptions in Act 2 Scene 3 and Act 3 Scene 1 are
forerunners to the main deception in Act 3 Scene 2 which leads to the
shaming and betrayal of Hero. For example, because we have seen
Beatrice and Benedick tricked, we are more ready to believe that Claudio
is similarly misled when he is persuaded by Don John that Hero was with
another man at her bedroom window.

1 a In pairs go through Act 2 Scene 3 and Act 3 Scene 1 and see how
many lines have a relevance to the later sinister deception of
Claudio by Don John in Act 3 Scene 2.
Example
**Claudio says 'Bait the hook well' (Act 2 Scene 3, line 105) which
is exactly what Don John later does to him.**
**Hero says 'I'll devise some honest slanders to stain my cousin
with' (Act 3 Scene 1, lines 84 to 85). Hero herself later becomes
the victim of a similar plan.**

b With your partner discuss the effect of these lines on the play.
Consider:

- How far do they set up the later deception of Claudio and
betrayal of Hero?
- Do they have an effect on the audience's view of these two
characters?

A CROSSROADS FOR BEATRICE AND BENEDICK

1 a Remembering the action and dialogue, particularly Beatrice and
Benedick's speeches at the end of the scenes where they decide to
love the other whole-heartedly (Act 2 Scene 3, lines 202 to 225
and Act 3 Scene 1, lines 107 to 116), write a diary entry for each
character as if written at the end of that day.

b In pairs improvise a scene which might occur on Beatrice and
Benedick's wedding day in which they read out these diary entries
to each other and talk about how they were helped to fall in love.

ACT 4, SCENE 1: THE SHAMING OF HERO

> Each activity in this section leads directly onto the next. However, it is possible to use any of them separately. The focus of the activities is on the dramatic irony in the scene.

1   Read the scene. In pairs write a short scene summary listing four to six important things which happen in the scene.

2   **a**   Divide the scene into the following three sections:

   - Section 1: line 1 to Claudio and Don Pedro's exit at line 108
   - Section 2: line 109 to Leonato and Hero's exit at line 250
   - Section 3: line 251 to the end of the scene.

   b   Choose one section to work on in pairs. Write out the most important lines, in effect summarising or shortening the section.

   c   All the pairs that have been working on section 1 should now come together to create a final version of that section of 10–20 lines. The pairs that have been working on sections 2 and 3 should do the same. At the end you should have a one- or two-page version of the scene.

3   **a**   Divide into three groups:

   - Group A: the actors (the characters in the scene)
   - Group B: the congregation
   - Group C: the audience

   b   Group A should decide who is going to play each character. Group B should decide on their character, e.g. Hero's childhood nurse. Group C should review the events that have led up to the wedding.

   c   In your groups discuss the expectations the different groups have of the wedding, e.g. the congregation might expect a lovely wedding but the audience might expect a disaster.

4 a For this activity you will need to set up a performance space. Think about the following questions:

- How do you imagine the church in which this scene takes place?
- What simple ideas can you come up with to create this environment in your classroom?
  Examples
  You could place a cross at one end of the room, or burn some incense to give the atmosphere of the church. The audience could sit at one end of the room, the congregation down the two sides of the room.

b In your 'church' perform your summarised version of the scene from activity 3.

c At the end discuss the reaction of the different groups compared to their expectations. For example, did the congregation witness the lovely wedding they were expecting?

d Perform the scene once more. This time someone should freeze the action occasionally to ask the reaction of members of the different groups.

5 Divide into three groups: groups A, B and C.

GROUP A

a Prepare a statement to the press/media from Leonato's household, announcing the death of Hero. Discuss how Leonato's household might want to present Hero's death. For example, would they want to encourage sympathy for Hero and hush up the allegations made by Claudio?

b Deliver your statement to the other two groups.

GROUP B

a Prepare a short improvisation involving members of the congregation gossiping to each other or to bystanders as they come out of the church. Think about whether they would sympathise with Claudio or with Hero as a member of the congregation. This can be very informal.
Example
You'll never guess what happened …

b Present this improvisation to the other two groups.

c Afterwards discuss the importance in the play of gossip. What examples can you think of?

GROUP C

a In the role of reporters, prepare questions for either Claudio or Don Pedro.
Examples
'Why did you decide to shame Hero in the church rather than quietly tell Leonato what you had seen?'
'Your friend Benedick has known Hero for some time – why did you not talk to him about your suspicions?'

b Now hold a press conference, with the actors who played Claudio and Don Pedro responding to the questions.

6 a Afterwards discuss the audience reaction to the actions of Claudio and Don Pedro in this scene. Consider these questions:

- Can the shaming of Hero be justified?
- Why did they accept the word of Don John, a known villain, so easily?
- Does Claudio love Hero or was he more interested in the fact that she is Leonato's only heir?
- Does Don Pedro have anything in common with Don John?

b Discuss the audience reaction to Beatrice and Benedick's belief in the innocence of Hero. How does this loyalty, perception and commitment to principle affect our hopes for their relationship?

ACT 4 SCENE 2: DOGBERRY AND THE SEXTON

Each activity in this section leads directly onto the next. However, it is possible to use any of them separately. The focus of the activities is on the contribution of the Watch to the tone and atmosphere of the play.

DOGBERRY AND THE COMEDY

The comedy in the scene comes from the bumbling, self-important Dogberry.

1 a In groups of five read through lines 1 to 33, taking the parts of Dogberry, Verges, Borachio, Conrade and the Sexton.

b Discuss the way you see the character of Dogberry. Consider these questions:

- What are his faults?
- What is the effect on the audience when he mixes up his words?
- How can we tell that he means well despite his arrogance and despite not knowing the first thing about questioning?
- How can we tell that he tries to do his job to the best of his ability?

2 a Think of one or two gestures that could be character traits for Dogberry, for example always standing up to speak or wagging his finger.

b In groups of five act out lines 1 to 33. The person playing Dogberry should make him a larger-than-life character and use the repeated gestures. Remember that Dogberry must not find himself funny. The more seriously he takes his job and himself the funnier the scene will be.

c Think about how the other characters in the scene should react to Dogberry. Act out lines 1 to 33 once more.

- The trusty Verges could nod approval at everything Dogberry says or does.
- The person playing the Sexton could show his frustration at Dogberry's incompetence whenever Dogberry does something wrong. For example, he could throw down his papers.

3 a The malapropisms (Dogberry's use of the wrong words, for example 'dissembly' instead of 'assembly' in line 1) are sometimes hard to recognise within the Shakespearean language. In groups of five, go through the scene identifying these words.

b Choose one group of five to play out the scene from line 1 to 33. The rest of the group should become the audience. Whenever Dogberry uses a word wrongly, the audience must call out the word that he should have used. The audience interaction should serve to highlight the frustration of the Sexton. The scene can be played with Dogberry ignoring the audience reaction or acknowledging it.

c In Shakespeare's time the audience may well have shouted out Dogberry's mistakes and Dogberry may well have pretended to be offended. Discuss ways in which an actor in a modern production could encourage the audience to participate in this way.

THE ACCUSATION

Most audiences love the character of Dogberry but we don't want his blustering to get in the way of the evidence coming to light – it may save Hero. The tone of the scene therefore changes when the watchmen are called to report what they overheard.

1 a In pairs read through lines 34 to 59, the Watch's report of Borachio's part in the shaming of Hero. Make a note of any evidence that would be useful for a future trial of Borachio and Conrade.

b Improvise a scene from this future trial. One of you should play the lawyer for the prosecution attempting to establish Borachio's guilt, the other should be Borachio. The lawyer should question Borachio and the accused, Borachio, must answer the questions.
Example questions:
'Did you receive from Don John the sum of one thousand ducats for accusing the lady wrongfully?'
'At the time that you took part in the deception did it occur to you that Claudio might shame Hero in the church?'

c In such a trial do you think Borachio and Conrade would plead guilty or not guilty?

2 The Sexton tells them: 'Prince John is this morning secretly stolen away. Hero was in this manner accused, in this very manner refused, and upon the grief of this suddenly died.' (lines 54 to 57)
Imagine that he added: 'What do you have to say to this?'

   a Consider these questions:

- Is this the first that Borachio and Conrade have heard of Hero being dead?
- How do you think they feel when they hear this?
- What might they have expected to happen at the wedding?
- How does Borachio feel about Don John stealing away?
- What punishments do they expect to receive?

   b In pairs write speeches for Borachio and Conrade replying to the Sexton's question 'What do you have to say to this?' How honest do you think they would be at this point in the play?

Dogberry's last speech

The audience are free to enjoy Dogberry's last speech (lines 67 to 79), knowing that the trick on Hero has been uncovered. Dogberry is outraged that Conrade called him an ass after the Sexton had left, and it will therefore not be recorded. His outrage grows throughout this speech.

1 Ten people should stand in a line. Each steps forward in turn saying a line as below. Each person must stress the 'and' that begins most lines and each must try to top the last person in volume and intensity.

   i)   I am a wise fellow
   ii)   and, which is more, an officer
   iii)   and, which is more, a householder
   iv)   and, which is more, as pretty a piece of flesh as any is in Messina
   v)   and one that knows the law, go to
   vi)   and a rich fellow, go to
   vii) and a fellow that hath had losses –
   viii) and one that hath two gowns and everything handsome about him
   ix)   Bring him away
   x)   O that I had been writ down an ass!

2 Discuss the character of Dogberry. Consider the following questions:

- What kind of comic skills does the actor playing Dogberry need?
- Why do audiences love the character of Dogberry?
- What does the character of Dogberry contribute to the play?

ACT 5 SCENE 1: THE CHALLENGE SCENE

Each activity leads directly onto the next, but it is possible to use any of them separately. The focus is on honour, honesty and social values.

LEONATO AND ANTONIO

After the events in the church, we expect the light-hearted world of Messina to have changed. For the old men it certainly has. The scene begins with Antonio trying to comfort Leonato who is tormented by what has happened. He now believes completely in Hero's innocence.

1 We never know what happened to Hero's mother, but we can presume that she is dead. After the betrayal of Hero Leonato might visit his wife's grave. Imagine that you are Leonato. Write a speech telling her what has happened. Consider:

- Does he feel guilt about not believing at first in Hero's innocence?
- How does he feel now about Don Pedro and Claudio?
- Does he blame himself for agreeing to the marriage?
- Does he imagine he can ever regain his past closeness with Hero?

2 When Claudio and Don Pedro arrive, their mood does not fit with the darker atmosphere in Messina. We expect that they have come to see Leonato having heard of Hero's 'death'. In fact, they are looking for Benedick, and they tell Leonato that they do not have time to talk.

a In groups of three write a 10-line scene in which Leonato and then Antonio issue a challenge to Claudio. You can use excerpts from the text (lines 46 to 109) or make up your own lines. Try to capture the atmosphere of the scene. There is some comedy in the aggression of two old men who would certainly find a fight difficult. Antonio is often played in productions as particularly frail to highlight this.
Example

Antonio   (Handing Claudio a glove, often the sign of a challenge) Take this, young man, and know that the hand that wields the sword is as strong.

Claudio   And as leathery! Take it back old man. Protect yourself from the sun. Your hands are dry enough ...

b Play out these scenes.

c As a group discuss the audience's feelings towards Claudio and Don Pedro after this incident.

BENEDICK

As soon as Leonato and Antonio have left to go back inside their house, Benedick arrives. It is a very different Benedick from the witty, lively young man we have seen in earlier scenes – he has undertaken the task of challenging Claudio, to kill or be killed by his best friend. Don Pedro and Claudio, in contrast, are the men they always were and try to get Benedick to use his wit to cheer them up. Benedick speaks plainly: 'You are a villain. I jest not.' (line 142) and issues his challenge because 'You have killed a sweet lady.' (lines 144 to 145) Still Claudio and Don Pedro persist in their banter, talking at length about how Beatrice has praised Benedick's wit. Benedick cuts them off, calling Claudio 'boy' and leaves them to their 'gossip-like humour' (lines 175 to 176).

1 a In pairs pick out three lines that are spoken by either Claudio or Don Pedro that seem to make Benedick particularly angry. Write down what Benedick might be thinking and why after each line.

b As a group discuss the audience's feelings towards Claudio and Don Pedro after this incident.

THE TRUTH COMES TO LIGHT

Dogberry and Verges enter with Borachio who confesses his and Don John's guilt to Claudio and Don Pedro. Meanwhile the Sexton is in the house with Leonato telling him that the 'trick' upon Hero has been uncovered. The truth is out.

1 In a production there is often an electric moment when Leonato and Antonio come from the house and the characters stand and look at each other for the first time since being in possession of the facts. The audience does not know what will happen next.

a Choose nine people to be the characters in this scene: Don Pedro, Claudio, Leonato, Antonio, the Sexton, Borachio, Conrade, Dogberry and Verges.

b As a group discuss the position you think the characters should take and model a freeze-frame of this moment. Who do you think each character would be looking at? For example, can Claudio look Leonato in the eyes?

c Once the characters are in position, ask each character what they are thinking and feeling at this moment, and what they expect to happen next.

2 a Read from line 244 to the end of the scene.

  b In pairs improvise a short scene which could take place after this scene, back in Leonato's house. One of you should play Hero and the other Leonato. Leonato tells her that Claudio has agreed to the new marriage. Consider the following questions:

- How do you think Hero feels about marrying Claudio this second time?
- How does she feel about pretending to be her own cousin?
- Do you think she has forgiven her father for not believing in her innocence at first?

3 a Read from line 244 to the end of the scene.

  b In pairs improvise a short scene which might take place after Claudio and Don Pedro have exited. One of you should play Claudio, and the other Don Pedro. You are discussing the events that have just taken place – the discovery that Hero was innocent and Leonato's offer of the new marriage. Remember that at this stage you still believe that Hero is dead. Consider the following questions:

- Claudio has expressed very little remorse in this scene. Is this really what he feels or is it a way to cope with his guilt?
Example
When Leonato said Claudio was guilty as well as Don John, Claudio replied 'Yet sinned I not but in mistaking.'
(lines 259 to 260)

- How responsible do you think Don Pedro feels for trusting his brother?

ACT 5 SCENE 4: THE FINAL SCENE – THE RESOLUTION

Each activity in this section leads directly onto the next. However, it is possible to use any of them separately. The focus of the activities is on discovering how complete the restoration of order is.

ATMOSPHERE

Much is glossed over in this short final scene. The reunion of Hero and Claudio and the union of Beatrice and Benedick both happen very quickly. The audience are often left with the feeling that the real resolving of the various issues will happen in the future. It is possible to stage this scene in different ways. For example, some productions give an uplifting feeling of mirth and joy, but others lay more stress on the tensions and issues still to be resolved.

1 a In pairs write a list of words that sum up the atmosphere that you would want to create in this scene if you were staging a production.

   b Consider these points:

   • How happy with the marriages would you want each character on stage to be? Make a list.
   • Tension on stage is caused by not knowing what might happen next. Make a list of the things that could happen that would overshadow the happiness at the end of the play.

HERO AND CLAUDIO

1 a Below is a list of lines that the characters say in the short section of the scene that brings Hero and Claudio together (lines 53 to 64). In groups of three write out the lines. Underneath each one, write down what you think the character is thinking at that moment in time.

CLAUDIO	Which is the lady I must seize upon?

ANTONIO	This same is she, and I do give you her.

CLAUDIO	Why, then she's mine. Sweet, let me see your face.

ANTONIO	No, that you shall not, till you take her hand Before this Friar, and swear to marry her.

CLAUDIO	Give me your hand: before this holy Friar, I am your husband, if you like of me.

HERO	(*Unmasking*) And when I lived, I was your other wife; And when you loved, you were my other husband.

CLAUDIO	Another Hero!

HERO	Nothing certainer. One Hero died defiled, but I do live; And surely as I live I am a maid.

b In your groups read through your scene, playing Hero, Claudio and Antonio. You should speak the lines from the text to each other and speak the characters' thoughts to an 'audience'.

2 Discuss what Claudio and Hero might be feeling. Consider the following questions:

- Is Hero criticising Claudio when she says 'when you loved' (line 61)
- How does Claudio feel when he is suddenly and unexpectedly face to face with the woman he shamed and hurt?

BEATRICE AND BENEDICK

In the short section of the scene in which Beatrice and Benedick come together they are finally defeated by their own actions. Using their usual witty banter, they deny their love for each other until letters are produced which prove their feelings. It is a public affair as they are coaxed on by the others, and it does more to re-establish the friendship of the group than the appearance of the real, and very much alive, Hero.

1 a Choose five people to play the roles of Beatrice, Benedick, Leonato, Claudio and Don Pedro. The rest of the group should form a circle around these characters.

b The characters should read the section of the scene from line 72 to line 97. The rest of the group should act as extra friends of the couple, and should call out to urge them on. The scene should end with a big cheer after Benedick's last line.

2 As a group, discuss the characters of Beatrice and Benedick and their roles in the play. You may want to consider these questions:

- What are the most important qualities that actors playing each of these roles should portray in the characters?
- How do you think that Beatrice and Benedick change throughout the play?
- What do the characters of Beatrice and Benedick contribute to the plot of the play?
- What effect do Beatrice and Benedick have on the characters around them?